DATE DUE

NOV 1 4 2011	
DEC 0 5 2012	
NOV 1 5 2013	

DEMCO, INC. 38-2971

Medical Ethics

Other Books in the Current Controversies Series

Medical Ethics

Noël Merino, Book Editor

GREENHAVEN PRESS
A part of Gale, Cengage Learning

Detroit • New York • San Francisco • New Haven, Conn • Waterville, Maine • London

Christine Nasso, *Publisher*
Elizabeth Des Chenes, *Managing Editor*

For more information, contact:
Greenhaven Press
27500 Drake Rd.
Farmington Hills, MI 48331-3535
Or you can visit our Internet site at gale.cengage.com

For product information and technology assistance, contact us at

Gale Customer Support, 1-800-877-4253
For permission to use material from this text or product, submit all requests online at
www.cengage.com/permissions

Further permissions questions can be emailed to permissionrequest@cengage.com

Articles in Greenhaven Press anthologies are often edited for length to meet page requirements. In addition, original titles of these works are changed to clearly present the main thesis and to explicitly indicate the author's opinion. Every effort is made to ensure that Greenhaven Press accurately reflects the original intent of the authors. Every effort has been made to trace the owners of copyrighted material.

Cover image copyright © Envision/Corbis.

LIBRARY OF CONGRESS CATALOGING-IN-PUBLICATION DATA

Medical ethics / Noël Merino, book editor.
    p. cm. -- (Current controversies)
    Includes bibliographical references and index.
    ISBN 978-0-7377-4915-1 (hardcover) -- ISBN 978-0-7377-4916-8 (pbk.)
    1. Medical ethics. I. Merino, Noël
    R724.M29274 2010
    174.2--dc22

                                                                2010015315

Printed in the United States of America
1 2 3 4 5 6 7 14 13 12 11 10

Contents

Chapter 1: What Ethics Should Guide the Health Care System?

Chapter 3: Are Reproductive Technologies Ethical?

There are good reasons why only married heterosexual couples, and not unmarried individuals and homosexuals, have a right to have a child.

Chapter 4: Is It Ethical for Doctors to End Life?

Yes: It Is Ethical for Doctors to End Life

Foreword

By definition, controversies are "discussions of questions in which opposing opinions clash" (Webster's Twentieth Century Dictionary Unabridged). Few would deny that controversies are a pervasive part of the human condition and exist on virtually every level of human enterprise. Controversies transpire between individuals and among groups, within nations and between nations. Controversies supply the grist necessary for progress by providing challenges and challengers to the status quo. They also create atmospheres where strife and warfare can flourish. A world without controversies would be a peaceful world; but it also would be, by and large, static and prosaic.

The Series' Purpose

The purpose of the Current Controversies series is to explore many of the social, political, and economic controversies dominating the national and international scenes today. Titles selected for inclusion in the series are highly focused and specific. For example, from the larger category of criminal justice, Current Controversies deals with specific topics such as police brutality, gun control, white collar crime, and others. The debates in Current Controversies also are presented in a useful, timeless fashion. Articles and book excerpts included in each title are selected if they contribute valuable, long-range ideas to the overall debate. And wherever possible, current information is enhanced with historical documents and other relevant materials. Thus, while individual titles are current in focus, every effort is made to ensure that they will not become quickly outdated. Books in the Current Controversies series will remain important resources for librarians, teachers, and students for many years.

In addition to keeping the titles focused and specific, great care is taken in the editorial format of each book in the series. Book introductions and chapter prefaces are offered to provide background material for readers. Chapters are organized around several key questions that are answered with diverse opinions representing all points on the political spectrum. Materials in each chapter include opinions in which authors clearly disagree as well as alternative opinions in which authors may agree on a broader issue but disagree on the possible solutions. In this way, the content of each volume in Current Controversies mirrors the mosaic of opinions encountered in society. Readers will quickly realize that there are many viable answers to these complex issues. By questioning each author's conclusions, students and casual readers can begin to develop the critical thinking skills so important to evaluating opinionated material.

Current Controversies is also ideal for controlled research. Each anthology in the series is composed of primary sources taken from a wide gamut of informational categories including periodicals, newspapers, books, U.S. and foreign government documents, and the publications of private and public organizations. Readers will find factual support for reports, debates, and research papers covering all areas of important issues. In addition, an annotated table of contents, an index, a book and periodical bibliography, and a list of organizations to contact are included in each book to expedite further research.

Perhaps more than ever before in history, people are confronted with diverse and contradictory information. During the Persian Gulf War, for example, the public was not only treated to minute-to-minute coverage of the war, it was also inundated with critiques of the coverage and countless analyses of the factors motivating U.S. involvement. Being able to sort through the plethora of opinions accompanying today's major issues, and to draw one's own conclusions, can be a complicated and frustrating struggle. It is the editors' hope that Current Controversies will help readers with this struggle.

Introduction

"The decision of Ashley's parents to administer the Ashley Treatment caused much controversy, with people for and against the decision."

Medical ethics is the study of ethics as it applies to medicine. Ethical issues that arise in the context of medicine include fundamental issues regarding access to necessary health care for basic preventive treatment on the one end and lifesaving organ transplant on the other end. With respect to medical treatments that are not necessary, ethical issues emerge regarding regulation, especially in the rapidly developing fields of genetic and reproductive technologies. With many of the ethical issues that surface in medicine, two of the key issues are patient autonomy—the right to choose and refuse treatment—and physician nonmaleficence—the expectation that doctors do no harm. A recent case discussed widely in the news media and medical ethics circles is that of the so-called Ashley Treatment.

Ashley X, whose last name has been withheld to protect the anonymity of the family, was born in 1997 with brain damage. She had what is known as static encephalopathy, which resulted in severe developmental disabilities that doctors predicted would keep her at the developmental level of an infant for her whole life. Since birth, Ashley has been unable to do anything on her own except to breathe. Her parents must move her and feed her through a tube. As Ashley grew older, her parents started to worry that caring for her would become increasingly difficult as she grew since "the chance of Ashley having significant improvement, such as being able to change her position in bed, let alone walk, is nonexistent."[1]

1. Ashley's Blog, "The 'Ashley Treatment,' Towards a Better Quality of Life for 'Pillow Angels,'" January 2, 2007. http://ashleytreatment.spaces.live.com/blog.

In 2004, when Ashley was six, her parents began looking into treatment to minimize her adult height and weight. They also wanted to eliminate her menstrual cycle and breast growth. The Ashley Treatment is the name doctors gave to a collection of medical procedures that, according to the parents, "together have the purpose of improving Ashley's quality of life and well-being."[2] Ashley received the Ashley Treatment on May 5, 2004, at Seattle Children's Hospital. The procedure included a hysterectomy, or removal of her uterus, to avoid menstruation and cramps; removal of her breast buds, to avoid breast growth; and appendectomy to avoid appendicitis, since Ashley cannot communicate being in pain. Shortly thereafter, she started high-dose estrogen therapy, which continued for two and a half years, to accelerate puberty with the goal of limiting Ashley's final height.

The decision of Ashley's parents to administer the Ashley Treatment caused much controversy, with people for and against the decision. Many people with disabilities expressed outrage at Ashley's parents' decision. The Disability Rights Education and Defense Fund argued against the treatment: "We hold as non-negotiable the principle that personal and physical autonomy of all people with disabilities be regarded as sacrosanct."[3] Ashley's parents defended their actions from disability activists in a 2008 interview, saying the criticism from disabled people "was based on their feelings about how inappropriate the treatment would be for them. Clearly, Ashley is in a vastly different category of disability than someone who is able to blog and write e-mails and can make decisions for themselves."[4]

Among bioethicists and medical professionals, the disagreement was just as great. Bioethicist Arthur Caplan argued

2. Ibid.

3. Disability Rights Education and Defense Fund, "Modify the System, Not the Person," January 7, 2007. http://dredf.org/news/ashley.shtml.

4. "'Pillow Angel' Parents Answer CNN's Questions," CNN.com, March 12, 2008. www.cnn.com.

that the Ashley Treatment is morally wrong: "Keeping Ashley small is a pharmacological solution for a social failure—the fact that American society does not do what it should to help severely disabled children and their families."[5] But physicians Daniel F. Gunther and Douglas S. Diekema, who performed the Ashley Treatment, claimed that "in situations in which parents request such an intervention, it is both medically feasible and ethically defensible."[6] In May 2007, Seattle Children's Hospital admitted it broke state law by giving Ashley a hysterectomy without a proper court review, although the hospital's ethics committee had approved the procedure.

Key issues of disagreement in the case of the Ashley Treatment were the extent to which Ashley's autonomy was respected and the extent to which the physicians were warranted in performing the treatment. Because of Ashley's mental disabilities, it was not possible to get her consent for the treatment. The crux of the disagreement among many people on this issue is whether her consent was needed and, if not, whether the treatment was in her best interest. As far as the appropriateness of performing the treatment, the disagreement centered largely on whether the treatment was helping or unnecessarily harming Ashley. These key issues arise in many other debates about medical ethics, a wide variety of which are explored in *Current Controversies: Medical Ethics.*

5. Arthur Caplan, "Is 'Peter Pan' Treatment a Moral Choice?" MSNBC.com, January 5, 2007. www.msnbc.msn.com.
6. Daniel F. Gunther and Douglas S. Diekema, "Attenuating Growth in Children with Profound Developmental Disability," *Archives of Pediatrics & Adolescent Medicine,* 2006. http://archpedi.ama-assn.org.

CHAPTER 1

What Ethics Should Guide the Health Care System?

Overview: The Health Care System

Public Agenda

Public Agenda is a nonpartisan, nonprofit organization that provides research to help American leaders understand the public's view and to help citizens know more about critical policy issues.

The nation's health care system is once again under the microscope as growing numbers of Americans are uninsured, costs keep rising, and the public grows increasingly worried about it.

Health Care in the United States

The U.S. spends more money on health care than any other nation. Health care spending will increase to $4.3 trillion by 2017, or $13,000 per person, according to the annual projection by the Centers for Medicare & Medicaid Services. Put another way, the rate of annual growth for health care will be 6.7 percent, which is three times the rate of inflation. Experts attribute the increase to higher demand for care and an aging population.

Yet higher spending on health care does not necessarily correspond to a healthier population, or even that everyone will get care. Some 47 million Americans go without health insurance, according to the Census Bureau, mostly people in jobs that don't offer it as an employee benefit. One-third of adults in the United States are obese, one of the highest rates in the world, according to the National Center for Health Statistics. Children too are increasingly overweight, contributing in part to the unprecedented levels of long-term health conditions like diabetes. And although Americans are indeed living longer than ever, the U.S. has been slipping in international rankings of life expectancy (it's currently at no. 42).

Countries rich and poor all struggle with how to provide affordable health care for their citizens without breaking the bank. Many countries, such as Canada and Britain, for example, have national health insurance programs, where the government provides health care. But the U.S. health care system is more market-driven, combining both private insurance and government programs.

The U.S. spends more on health care than any other nation.

Most Americans (about six in 10) get their health coverage as an employee benefit. As a result, the number of uninsured people tends to swing up and down with the economy, as employers lay off or cut back in hard times. Low-income people and young adults are most likely to be uninsured. Those without insurance are 25 percent more likely to die during any given year than those with insurance. And of course, even though people with employer-provided insurance only pay a fraction of their health costs, it's far from free—the Kaiser Family Foundation reports the average family premium is more than $12,000 per year, of which employees pay roughly one-quarter.

The government does play a major role in providing health care, through programs for the elderly (Medicare), the poor (Medicaid) and low-income children, as well as through veterans benefits and insurance for federal employees and their families. In fact, the federal government currently pays for more than 40 percent of the nation's health care bills. The government also provides substantial tax breaks ($225 billion total) for employers who provide insurance.

People who aren't covered by an employer or the government can still buy health coverage from an insurance company on their own—but relatively few do. Individuals end up paying the highest rates, because businesses usually negotiate a cheaper group rate.

Proposals to Cut Health Costs

Some proposals to rein in health costs include embracing a free-market approach to make the insurance marketplace more competitive and less expensive by using tax credits to encourage more people to buy health insurance on their own instead of receiving it from their employers. Supporters say one reason expenses are rising is that it's hard for most people to tell how much their health care really costs. Most people who have insurance only pay part of the cost through co-pays, deductibles or employee contributions—the insurance company pays the rest, and the patient may or may not ever see a bill. And since different insurance plans negotiate different deals with providers, the bills for two people with the same illness could be quite different. Many experts say that since the patient isn't bearing the real cost, there's no incentive to control costs.

More than half of Americans say they are dissatisfied with the quality of health care in the U.S.

Other experts say the only real way to tame health care costs is to do what Canada and many European countries have done by going to a government "single-payer" plan, something that might work like Medicare or Medicaid, but would cover everyone. Advocates say this will cut costs because the government could eliminate the inefficiency in our current mixed system and use its enormous purchasing power to get the best deals. Opponents say this would wipe out private insurance and leave employers and patients with less control over their coverage.

In the absence of any national health insurance, some states and municipalities are taking action themselves to provide universal coverage: San Francisco, for example, offers free or subsidized health care to all city adults without insurance. Since 2007, Massachusetts has required residents to have health insurance, with state subsidies available to make it affordable for low-income residents.

The Public Voice

On this issue, the attitudes of many Americans are a bundle of contradictions, which is an indication that, on many issues, the public has not yet "worked through" their views. Majorities say the health care system needs to be fundamentally changed, and most say it is the government's responsibility to ensure everyone has adequate health care coverage. But responses vary when faced with the potential costs and trade-offs of a universal health care system.

Access to health care and its costs now top Americans' perceptions of the most urgent health problem facing the country today, a marked change from two decades ago when AIDS ranked first on the list of the nation's health problems, and virtually no one mentioned access or costs.

More than half of Americans say they are dissatisfied with the quality of health care in the U.S. Most say HMOs [health maintenance organizations] and other managed care programs have decreased the quality of care, and a majority says HMOs do a bad job serving their customers. Yet most Americans belong to managed care plans, and the vast majority report receiving good or excellent care for themselves and their families.

Rationing Health Care Is Ethical and Necessary

Peter Singer

Peter Singer is the Ira W. DeCamp Professor of Bioethics at Princeton University and laureate professor at the Centre for Applied Philosophy and Public Ethics at the University of Melbourne. He is the author of Practical Ethics.

You have advanced kidney cancer. It will kill you, probably in the next year or two. A drug called Sutent slows the spread of the cancer and may give you an extra six months, but at a cost of $54,000. Is a few more months worth that much?

If you can afford it, you probably would pay that much, or more, to live longer, even if your quality of life wasn't going to be good. But suppose it's not you with the cancer but a stranger covered by your health insurance fund. If the insurer provides this man—and everyone else like him—with Sutent, your premiums will increase. Do you still think the drug is a good value? Suppose the treatment costs a million dollars. Would it be worth it then? Ten million? Is there any limit to how much you would want your insurer to pay for a drug that adds six months to someone's life? If there is any point at which you say, "No, an extra six months isn't worth that much," then you think that health care should be rationed. . . .

The Issue of Rationing

Rationing health care means getting value for the billions we are spending by setting limits on which treatments should be paid for from the public purse. If we ration we won't be writing blank checks to pharmaceutical companies for their patented drugs, nor paying for whatever procedures doctors choose to recommend. When public funds subsidize health care or provide it directly, it is crazy not to try to get value for money. The debate over health care reform in the United States should start from the premise that some form of health care rationing is both inescapable and desirable. Then we can ask, What is the best way to do it?

Last year [2008] Britain's National Institute for Health and Clinical Excellence [NICE] gave a preliminary recommendation that the National Health Service should not offer Sutent for advanced kidney cancer. The institute, generally known as NICE, is a government-financed but independently run organization set up to provide national guidance on promoting good health and treating illness. The decision on Sutent did not, at first glance, appear difficult. NICE had set a general limit of £30,000, or about $49,000, on the cost of extending life for a year. Sutent, when used for advanced kidney cancer, cost more than that, and research suggested it offered only about six months extra life. But the British media leapt on the theme of penny-pinching bureaucrats sentencing sick people to death. The issue was then picked up by the U.S. news media and by those lobbying against health care reform in the United States. An article in the *New York Times* last December featured Bruce Hardy, a kidney-cancer patient whose wife, Joy, said, "It's hard to know that there is something out there that could help but they're saying you can't have it because of cost." Then she asked the classic question: "What price is life?"

The debate over health care reform in the United States should start from the premise that some form of health care rationing is both inescapable and desirable.

Last November, Bloomberg News focused on Jack Rosser, who was 57 at the time and whose doctor had told him that with Sutent he might live long enough to see his 1-year-old daughter, Emma, enter primary school. Rosser's wife, Jenny, is quoted as saying: "It's immoral. They are sentencing him to die." In the conservative monthly the *American Spectator*, David Catron, a health care consultant, describes Rosser as "one of NICE's many victims" and writes that NICE "regularly hands down death sentences to gravely ill patients." Linking the British system with Democratic proposals for reforming health care in the United States, Catron asked whether we really deserve a health care system in which "soulless bureaucrats arbitrarily put a dollar value on our lives." (In March, NICE issued a final ruling on Sutent. Because of how few patients need the drug and because of special end-of-life considerations, it recommended that the drug be provided by the National Health Service to patients with advanced kidney cancer.)

The Ability to Pay

There's no doubt that it's tough—politically, emotionally and ethically—to make a decision that means that someone will die sooner than they would have if the decision had gone the other way. But if the stories of Bruce Hardy and Jack Rosser lead us to think badly of the British system of rationing health care, we should remind ourselves that the U.S. system also results in people going without lifesaving treatment—it just does so less visibly. Pharmaceutical manufacturers often charge much more for drugs in the United States than they charge for the same drugs in Britain, where they know that a higher price would put the drug outside the cost-effectiveness limits set by NICE. American patients, even if they are covered by Medicare or Medicaid, often cannot afford the co-payments for drugs. That's rationing too, by ability to pay.

Dr. Art Kellermann, associate dean for public policy at Emory [University] School of Medicine in Atlanta, recently wrote of a woman who came into his emergency room in critical condition because a blood vessel had burst in her brain. She was uninsured and had chosen to buy food for her children instead of spending money on her blood pressure medicine. In the emergency room, she received excellent high-tech medical care, but by the time she got there, it was too late to save her.

The U.S. system also results in people going without life-saving treatment.

A *New York Times* report on the high costs of some drugs illustrates the problem. Chuck Stauffer, an Oregon farmer, found that his prescription-drug insurance left him to pay $5,500 for his first 42 days of Temodar, a drug used to treat brain tumors, and $1,700 a month after that. For Medicare patients drug costs can be even higher, because Medicare can require a co-payment of 25 percent of the cost of the drug. For Gleevec, a drug that is effective against some forms of leukemia and some gastrointestinal tumors, that one-quarter of the cost can run to $40,000 a year.

The Uninsured

In Britain, everyone has health insurance. In the U.S., some 45 million do not, and nor are they entitled to any health care at all, unless they can get themselves to an emergency room. Hospitals are prohibited from turning away anyone who will be endangered by being refused treatment. But even in emergency rooms, people without health insurance may receive less health care than those with insurance. Joseph Doyle, a professor of economics at the Sloan School of Management at MIT [Massachusetts Institute of Technology], studied the records of people in Wisconsin who were injured in severe automobile accidents and had no choice but to go to the hospital. He estimated that those who had no health insurance received 20 percent less care and had a death rate 37 percent higher than those with health insurance. This difference held up even when those without health insurance were compared with those without automobile insurance, and with those on Medicaid—groups with whom they share some characteristics that might affect treatment. The lack of insurance seems to be what caused the greater number of deaths.

Estimates of the number of U.S. deaths caused annually by the absence of universal health insurance go as high as 20,000.

When the media feature someone like Bruce Hardy or Jack Rosser, we readily relate to individuals who are harmed by a government agency's decision to limit the cost of health care. But we tend not to hear about—and thus don't identify with—the particular individuals who die in emergency rooms because they have no health insurance. This "identifiable victim" effect, well documented by psychologists, creates a dangerous bias in our thinking. Doyle's figures suggest that if those Wisconsin accident victims without health insurance had received equivalent care to those with it, the additional health care would have cost about $220,000 for each life saved. Those who died were on average around 30 years old and could have been expected to live for at least another 40 years; this means that had they survived their accidents, the cost per extra year of life would have been no more than $5,500—a small fraction of the $49,000 that NICE recommends the British National Health Service should be ready to pay to give a patient an extra year of life. If the U.S. system spent less on expensive treatments for those who, with or without the drugs, have at most a few months to live, it would be better able to save the lives of more people who, if they get the treatment they need, might live for several decades.

Estimates of the number of U.S. deaths caused annually by the absence of universal health insurance go as high as 20,000. One study concluded that in the age group 55 to 64 alone, more than 13,000 extra deaths a year may be attributed to the lack of insurance coverage. But the estimates vary because Americans without health insurance are more likely, for example, to smoke than Americans with health insurance, and sorting out the role that the lack of insurance plays is difficult. Richard Kronick, a professor at the School of Medicine at the University of California, San Diego, cautiously concludes from his own study that there is little evidence to suggest that extending health insurance to all Americans would have a large effect on the number of deaths in the United States. That doesn't mean that it wouldn't; we simply don't know if it would. . . .

The Value of Human Life

When a *Washington Post* journalist asked Daniel Zemel, a Washington rabbi, what he thought about federal agencies putting a dollar value on human life, the rabbi cited a Jewish teaching explaining that if you put one human life on one side of a scale, and you put the rest of the world on the other side, the scale is balanced equally. Perhaps that is how those who resist health care rationing think. But we already put a dollar value on human life. If the Department of Transportation, for example, followed rabbinical teachings it would exhaust its entire budget on road safety. Fortunately, the department sets a limit on how much it is willing to pay to save one human life. In 2008 that limit was $5.8 million. Other government agencies do the same. Last year the Consumer Product Safety Commission considered a proposal to make mattresses less likely to catch fire. Information from the industry suggested that the new standard would cost $343 million to implement, but the Consumer Product Safety Commission calculated that it would save 270 lives a year—and since it valued a human life at around $5 million, that made the new standard a good value. If we are going to have consumer-safety regulation at all, we need some idea of how much safety is worth buying. Like health care bureaucrats, consumer-safety bureaucrats sometimes decide that saving a human life is not worth the expense. Twenty years ago, the National Research Council, an arm of the National Academy of Sciences, examined a proposal for installing seat belts in all school buses. It estimated that doing so would save, on average, one life per year, at a cost of $40 million. After that, support for the proposal faded away. So why is it that those who accept that we put a price on life when it comes to consumer safety refuse to accept it when it comes to health care?

Of course, it's one thing to accept that there's a limit to how much we should spend to save a human life, and another to set that limit. The dollar value that bureaucrats place on a generic human life is intended to reflect social values, as revealed in our behavior. It is the answer to the question "How much are you willing to pay to save your life?"—except that, of course, if you asked that question of people who were facing death, they would be prepared to pay almost anything to save their lives. So instead, economists note how much people are prepared to pay to reduce the risk that they will die. How much will people pay for air bags in a car, for instance? Once you know how much they will pay for a specified reduction in risk, you multiply the amount that people are willing to pay by how much the risk has been reduced, and then you know, or so the theory goes, what value people place on their lives. Suppose that there is a 1 in 100,000 chance that an air bag in my car will save my life, and that I would pay $50—but no more than that—for an air bag. Then it looks as if I value my life at $50 x 100,000, or $5 million.

The theory sounds good, but in practice it has problems. We are not good at taking account of differences between very small risks, so if we are asked how much we would pay to reduce a risk of dying from 1 in 1,000,000 to 1 in 10,000,000, we may give the same answer as we would if asked how much we would pay to reduce the risk from 1 in 500,000 to 1 in

10,000,000. Hence multiplying what we would pay to reduce the risk of death by the reduction in risk lends an apparent mathematical precision to the outcome of the calculation—the supposed value of a human life—that our intuitive responses to the questions cannot support. Nevertheless this approach to setting a value on a human life is at least closer to what we really believe—and to what we should believe—than dramatic pronouncements about the infinite value of every human life, or the suggestion that we cannot distinguish between the value of a single human life and the value of a million human lives, or even of the rest of the world. Though such feel-good claims may have some symbolic value in particular circumstances, to take them seriously and apply them—for instance, by leaving it to chance whether we save one life or a billion—would be deeply unethical.

It's one thing to accept that there's a limit to how much we should spend to save a human life, and another to set that limit.

Governments implicitly place a dollar value on a human life when they decide how much is to be spent on health care programs and how much on other public goods that are not directed toward saving lives. The task of health care bureaucrats is then to get the best value for the resources they have been allocated. It is the familiar comparative exercise of getting the most bang for your buck. Sometimes that can be relatively easy to decide. If two drugs offer the same benefits and have similar risks of side effects, but one is much more expensive than the other, only the cheaper one should be provided by the public health care program. That the benefits and the risks of side effects are similar is a scientific matter for experts to decide after calling for submissions and examining them. That is the bread-and-butter work of units like NICE. But the benefits may vary in ways that defy straightforward comparison. We need a common unit for measuring the goods achieved by health care. Since we are talking about comparing different goods, the choice of unit is not merely a scientific or economic question but an ethical one.

The Quality-Adjusted Life-Year

As a first take, we might say that the good achieved by health care is the number of lives saved. But that is too crude. The death of a teenager is a greater tragedy than the death of an 85-year-old, and this should be reflected in our priorities. We can accommodate that difference by calculating the number of life-years saved, rather than simply the number of lives saved. If a teenager can be expected to live another 70 years, saving her life counts as a gain of 70 life-years, whereas if a person of 85 can be expected to live another 5 years, then saving the 85-year-old will count as a gain of only 5 life-years. That suggests that saving one teenager is equivalent to saving 14 85-year-olds. These are, of course, generic teenagers and generic 85-year-olds. It's easy to say, "What if the teenager is a violent criminal and the 85-year-old is still working productively?" But just as emergency rooms should leave criminal justice to the courts and treat assailants and victims alike, so decisions about the allocation of health care resources should be kept separate from judgments about the moral character or social value of individuals.

Health care does more than save lives: It also reduces pain and suffering. How can we compare saving a person's life with, say, making it possible for someone who was confined to bed to return to an active life? We can elicit people's values on that too. One common method is to describe medical conditions to people—let's say being a quadriplegic—and tell them that they can choose between 10 years in that condition or some smaller number of years without it. If most would prefer, say, 10 years as a quadriplegic to 4 years of nondisabled life, but would choose 6 years of nondisabled life over 10 with quadriplegia, but have difficulty deciding between 5 years of nondisabled life or 10 years with quadriplegia, then they are, in effect, assessing life with quadriplegia as half as good as nondisabled life. (These are hypothetical figures, chosen to keep the math simple, and not based on any actual surveys.) If that judgment represents a rough average across the population, we might conclude that restoring to nondisabled life two people who would otherwise be quadriplegics is equivalent in value to saving the life of one person, provided the life expectancies of all involved are similar.

The death of a teenager is a greater tragedy than the death of an 85-year-old, and this should be reflected in our priorities.

This is the basis of the quality-adjusted life-year, or QALY, a unit designed to enable us to compare the benefits achieved by different forms of health care. The QALY has been used by economists working in health care for more than 30 years to compare the cost-effectiveness of a wide variety of medical procedures and, in some countries, as part of the process of deciding which medical treatments will be paid for with public money. If a reformed U.S. health care system explicitly accepted rationing, as I have argued it should, QALYs could play a similar role in the U.S. . . . .

The QALY is not a perfect measure of the good obtained by health care, but its defenders can support it in the same way that Winston Churchill defended democracy as a form of government: It is the worst method of allocating health care, except for all the others. If it isn't possible to provide everyone with all beneficial treatments, what better way do we have of deciding what treatments people should get than by comparing the QALYs gained with the expense of the treatments?

Health Care Rationing Should Not Be Justified by Unethical Beliefs

Raymond Dennehy

Raymond Dennehy is professor of philosophy at the University of San Francisco. He is the author of Anti-Abortionist at Large: How to Argue Intelligently About Abortion and Live to Tell About It.

Peter Singer's current op-ed piece in the *New York Times Magazine* [July 19, 2009], "Why We Must Ration Health Care," is timely, all the more so since the Congressional Budget Office now estimates that President Barack Obama's health care plan will cost $1.5 trillion more than the White House estimate. Singer notes that in the debate over health care reform, "rationing" has become a dirty word. His essay doesn't attempt to tidy the word up, but only to persuade readers that health care reform is the only solution to the nation's health care problems and that you can't have successful reform without rationing.

Singer's Argument for Rationing

Singer's approach here is not his classic vintage. There's no advocacy, let alone mention, of procedures, such as infant euthanasia, that have made his name a national brand for academically sponsored evil. But just as the "Lite" version of a beverage can be as harmful as the "Classic" version, we would be rash to assume that "Singer Lite" is healthier for America than "Singer Classic."

Singer argues that all scarce resources are "rationed in one way or another," and health care is a scarce resource. If your

Raymond Dennehy, "The Right (and Wrong) Way To Ration Health Care," *OSV Newsweekly*, August 9, 2009. Reproduced by permission.

health care plan is privately financed, which it usually is, we're talking about "rationing by price," since the plan we have depends on what we or our employer can afford to pay. And in the case of Medicare, Medicaid and hospital emergency rooms, "health care is rationed by long waits, high patient co-payment requirements, low payments to doctors that discourage some from serving public patients and limits on payments to hospitals."

Singer is right about the inevitability of rationing when medical and fiscal resources are scarce.

In addition, health care premiums have doubled in the past decade and are increasing four times faster than wages. According to Medicare trustees, the program's major fund will be bankrupt in eight years. Even privately insured Americans are finding that they can't afford treatment.

All of which is designed to convince us that explicit rationing is the only way to guarantee that Medicare and Medicaid can keep on providing adequate medical care to its subscribers. Singer is right about the inevitability of rationing when medical and fiscal resources are scarce. It would be imprudent to squander scarce medical resources on patients that are bad bets for successful outcomes. It makes sense that, if bodily organs are in short supply, a 70-year-old patient in need of a liver transplant should be bypassed in favor of the 20-year-old patient.

Weighing Human Life

But here's where you have to ask whether "Singer Lite" is any better for our democratic values than "Singer Classic." Since rationing medical care requires pitting the needs of one patient against what is good for the majority of patients, how does Singer meet the objection that it is impossible to weigh the value of a single human life against the value of the whole

33

human race? He responds by saying that taking such "feel-good claims" seriously is "deeply unethical."

All right-thinking folks would agree that one shouldn't do what is unethical, let alone what is "deeply unethical." But what one calls "ethical" depends on which moral theory one embraces. Singer is a utilitarian, and a core principle of the utilitarian ethic is that no act is moral or immoral in itself but only in its consequences; accordingly, the goal of action is to produce a balance of benefits over harms.

Thus in his book, *Practical Ethics*, he proposes a "deeply ethical" behavior in his defense of infanticide: "When the death of a disabled infant will lead to the birth of another infant with better prospects of a happy life, the total amount of happiness will be greater if the disabled infant is killed. The loss of happy life for the first infant is outweighed by the gain of a happier life for the second. Therefore, if killing the hemophiliac infant has no adverse effect on others, it would, according to the total view, be right to kill him." Singer offers a similar remedy for infants with spina bifida and Down syndrome. How's that for slashing health costs?

Prudence dictates that the ethical theory of those who would decide who gets treatment and who does not be kept in full view while evaluating Singer's proposed basis for making those decisions: "quality-adjusted life-year, or QALY." This is a unit that allows a comparison between the benefits offered by different forms of health care. It is a tool that economists in the health care field use to compare the cost-effectiveness of different medical procedures.

The value of the human person and his right to life do not depend on features that make men different.

Assuming, he says, that "a year with quadriplegia is valued at only half as much as a year without it, then treatment that extends the lives of people without disabilities will be seen as providing twice the value of one that extends, for a similar period, the lives of quadriplegics. That clashes with the idea that all human lives are of equal value."

The Value of Human Nature

Singer believes using cases like this to safeguard the claim that everyone has an equal right to life is a sword that cuts both ways: "If life with quadriplegia is as good as life without it, there is no health benefit to be gained by curing it. . . . Disability advocates, it seems, are forced to choose between insisting that extending their lives is just as important as extending the lives of people without disabilities, and seeking public support for research into a cure for their condition."

The kind of contrast that Singer draws between lives with disabilities and lives without them collides with the doctrine of natural rights that forms the bedrock of our democracy. The basis of life, liberty and the pursuit of happiness is human nature, and a disabled person has not lost that nature. To borrow from the philosopher, Yves R. Simon, it is just as much an act of murder to kill a sickly man as a healthy one; it is just as much an act of murder to kill a colored man as a white man; it is just as much an act of murder to kill a poor man as a rich man; it is just as much an act of murder to kill a child in its mother's womb as a human adult.

The value of the human person and his right to life do not depend on features that make men different, but rather on the essential features of personhood that are common to all human beings.

But Singer is not only consistent with his utilitarian ethics, he is also consistent with his materialism. He has made no secret of his belief that human beings are not sacrosanct, not preeminent in nature. Our belief that they are has, he insists, produced more harm than good. Not surprisingly, he regards it just as immoral to torture a puppy as a human baby.

Ultimately, the proposals of "Singer Lite" for rationing health care may be as toxic as those of "Singer Classic."

Universal Health Care Provided by the Government Is Morally Required

New Republic

The New Republic *is an online and print magazine that examines American politics, foreign policy, and culture.*

Over the last 25 years, liberalism has lost both its good name and its sway over politics. But it is liberalism's loss of imagination that is most disheartening. Since President [Bill] Clinton's health care plan unraveled in 1994—a debacle that this magazine, regrettably, abetted—liberals have grown chastened and confused, afraid to think big ideas. Such reticence had its proper time and place; large-scale political and substantive failures demand introspection, not to mention humility. But it is time to be ambitious again. And the place to begin is the very spot where liberalism left off a decade ago: Guaranteeing every American citizen access to affordable, high-quality medical care.

The Hardships of the Uninsured

The familiar name for this idea is "universal health care," a term that, however accurate, drains the concept of its moral resonance. Alone among the most developed nations, the United States allows nearly 16 percent of its population—46 million people—to go without health insurance. And, while it is commonly assumed that the uninsured still get medical care, statistics and anecdotes tell a different story. Across the United States today, there are diabetics skimping on their insulin, child asthmatics struggling to breathe, and cancer victims dying from undetected tumors. Studies by the Institute of Medicine suggest that thousands of people, maybe even tens of thousands, die prematurely every year because they don't have health insurance. And even those who don't suffer medical consequences face financial and emotional pain, as when seniors choose between prescriptions and groceries—or when families choose between the mortgage and hospital bills.

These are not the sorts of hardships that an enlightened society tolerates, particularly when those hardships so frequently visit people who, as the politicians like to say, "work hard and play by the rules." Yet American society has tolerated this situation for a long time. It has done so, at least in part, because the majority of working Americans still had private health insurance, generally through their jobs—the consequences of losing health coverage were, for the most part, somebody else's concern. Universal health care promised them security they already had. Change would only be for the worse.

Alone among the most developed nations, the United States allows nearly 16 percent of its population—46 million people—to go without health insurance.

A Lack of Health Care Security

But how many people can really count upon such security now? Precisely because working people expect to get insurance through their jobs, they are dependent upon the enthusiasm of employers to help pay for it—an enthusiasm that is waning in the face of rising medical costs and global competition. Companies have responded by reengineering their workforces to shed full-time workers that receive benefits, by redesigning their insurance plans to offer skimpier coverage, or by simply declining to offer coverage altogether. Soon, the only employers left offering generous health coverage may be the ones forced to do so by union contracts—employers like the Big

Three automakers [General Motors, Ford, and Chrysler], which, when we last checked, were barely skirting bankruptcy themselves.

When such gaps in insurance have appeared previously in U.S. history, the government has stepped in to fill them. It did so most audaciously in the 1960s, when the Great Society produced Medicare and Medicaid in order to guarantee at least some coverage to the elderly and the poor—groups the employer-based system had repeatedly failed to serve. But chronically underfunded Medicaid, a program that never reached all of the uninsured, cannot accommodate the growing demand when conservatives keep cutting taxes and gutting public services. Combined with the decline of employer-sponsored coverage, this failure means that even middle-class Americans are just one downsizing away from losing health insurance altogether.

An Ill-Functioning Health Care System

Such widespread insecurity might be understandable (though not necessarily forgivable) if it were the unavoidable consequence of an otherwise well-functioning health care system. After all, economics teaches us that trade-offs between efficiency and equity are inevitable. But medical care in this country is inequitable and inefficient. The United States pays more for its health care than any other nation on the planet: 16 percent of our national wealth, at last count. Money spent on health care is money not spent on other things, like corporate investment and wages. That's an exorbitant cost that even Americans with secure health insurance pay.

"Exorbitant," to be sure, is a subjective word: Money spent on well-applied medical technology might be worth it. But, perversely, our extra spending doesn't seem to buy us better medical care. According to virtually every meaningful statistic, from simple measures like infant mortality to more carefully constructed data like "potential years of life lost," Americans are no healthier (and are frequently unhealthier) than the citizens of countries with universal health care. Nor do Americans always get "more" medical care, as is commonly assumed. The citizens of Japan, for example, have more CT scanners and MRI machines than we do. And the French, whose system the World Health Organization recently declared the planet's best, have more hospital beds. They get more doctor visits, too, perhaps because their access to physicians is nearly unfettered—a privilege even most middle-class Americans surrendered with the spread of managed care. In fact, aside from cost, the measure on which the United States most conspicuously stands out from other advanced nations may be public opinion: In a series of polls a few years ago, just 40 percent of us said we were "fairly or very" satisfied with our health care system, fourth worst of the 17 nations surveyed. . . .

A Right, Not a Privilege

It's time for the government to be much bolder, to try something even more far-reaching than what it attempted in the '60s: making health care a right, not a privilege. And doing so for everybody, even if that means having the government provide insurance directly. Such a proposal might confound the conventional notions about what works and what doesn't work in public policy. But providing health insurance happens to be a job the public sector has already proved it can do very well. The most popular health insurance plan in the United States is Medicare—which, except for the drug benefit and a few HMOs [health maintenance organizations] that contract for the business, is a government-run health care program. And Medicare isn't only popular. It's also efficient. Nearly all of the money that goes into the program, via taxes and the premiums seniors pay, goes back out to purchase actual medical services. Private insurance, by contrast, inevitably diverts a much greater share of its premium dollars to administration, marketing, and profits, which means less money for the beneficiaries. In theory, insurance companies should be competing to provide their subscribers with the best, most cost-effective medical care. In practice, they compete over who can enroll the healthiest patients, since that is the surest way to improve profit margins.

Medical care in this country is inequitable and inefficient.

The other reason universal health care may seem an unconventional suggestion is because it is an "old" idea. The first proposals for universal health care surfaced at the end of the Progressive Era, nearly a century ago. But "old" is not the same thing as "bad," and time has only made universal health care more relevant, not less. During the twentieth century, this country saved capitalism not only from its foes abroad, but also from its deficiencies at home—chief among them its tendency to visit catastrophe on a few unlucky souls. While the foreign threat to capitalism has subsided, the domestic inadequacies are becoming severe once again, as pensions and job security vanish in the hypercompetitive global economy. The historic solution to this problem was to insulate individuals from excessive risk. And, while the private sector once did this for health care, it's no longer up to the task. Government isn't the best way to provide all Americans with health security. It's the only way. And it's time for liberalism to say so openly.

Government Intervention in Health Care Is Immoral and Impractical

Lin Zinser and Paul Hsieh

Lin Zinser is founder of Freedom and Individual Rights in Medicine (FIRM), an organization dedicated to education and intellectual activism regarding the causes of and solutions to the current problems with health insurance and medicine. Paul Hsieh is a practicing diagnostic radiologist in Denver and a founding member of FIRM.

Although American scientists, doctors, and businessmen have produced the most advanced medical technology in the world, American health care is in a state of crisis. Technologically, we are surrounded by medical marvels: New "clot buster" drugs enable patients to survive heart attacks that once would have been fatal; new forms of "keyhole surgery" enable patients with appendicitis to be treated and discharged within twenty-four hours, whereas previously they would have spent a week in the hospital; advances in cancer treatment enabled bicyclist Lance Armstrong to beat a testicular cancer, which, had he lived fifty years ago, would have killed him; and so on.

The Need for Health Care Reform

From an economic perspective, however, such medical treatments are increasingly out of reach to many Americans. Health care costs, as reported by the *New York Times*, are rising twice as fast as inflation. And health insurance, as reported by *USA Today*, "is becoming increasingly unaffordable for many em-

Lin Zinser and Paul Hsieh, "Moral Health Care vs. 'Universal Health Care,'" *Objective Standard*, vol. 2, no. 4, Winter 2007–2008. Copyright © 2007–2008 The Objective Standard. All Rights Reserved. Reproduced by permission.

ployers and working people." A decreasing percentage of employers are offering health insurance benefits to their workers, and many of those who are offering benefits are requiring their employees to pay a greater percentage of the costs. The U.S. Census Bureau reported in 2007 that nearly forty-seven million Americans had no health insurance, a sharp increase of ten million people from a mere fifteen years earlier. In short, there is a major disconnect between existing lifesaving medical technology and the ability of Americans to afford it.

This discord is affecting doctors as well. The American Medical Association warns physicians that, due to the lack of affordable health insurance, "more patients will delay treatment and . . . doctors will likely see more uncompensated care." Hence, each year doctors are working harder and harder but making less and less money, resulting in a "critical level" of stress and burnout. According to a recent survey of doctors, "30 to 40 percent of practicing physicians would not choose to enter the medical profession if they were deciding on a career again, and an even higher percentage would not encourage their children to pursue a medical career."

Government interference in medicine has caused incalculable harm to both patients and doctors, and driven up the cost of health care.

Total spending on health care in the United States amounts to nearly 17 percent of the entire economy, and this is expected to rise to 20 percent by 2015, "with annual spending consistently growing faster than the overall economy." Because of skyrocketing health care costs, the U.S. federal Medicare trust fund is expected to go bankrupt in 2019, less than twelve years from now [2007], potentially leaving millions of elderly Americans without health insurance coverage. American health care is in dire straits and will continue to worsen—unless Americans demand fundamental political change to reverse the trend. Unfortunately, the kinds of changes currently being proposed by politicians will only exacerbate the problem.

The Proposal for Universal Health Care

Politicians from across the political spectrum, including [2008] Democratic presidential candidate Hillary Clinton and Republican candidate Mitt Romney, have argued that the government should guarantee "universal coverage" to all Americans, making health care a "right." And politicians are not alone; numerous businessmen, union leaders, and insurance executives are united in saying that this will solve our problems.

Charity already abounds in America and would be even more abundant if the government removed its coercive hands.

It will not.

Contrary to claims that government-imposed "universal health care" would solve America's health care problems, it would in fact destroy American medicine and countless lives along with it. The goal of "universal health care" (a euphemism for socialized medicine) is both immoral and impractical; it violates the rights of businessmen, doctors, and patients to act on their own judgment—which, in turn, throttles their ability to produce, administer, or purchase the goods and services in question. . . .

A Genuine Solution

The solution to America's health care problems is not more government intervention. Government violations of individual rights through government interference in the marketplace are the source of the problems. Government meddling in health insurance has all but eliminated choice, competition, and innovation, and has driven up the cost of health insurance.

Government interference in medicine has caused incalculable harm to both patients and doctors, and driven up the cost of health care. Government controls have bred more controls, as politicians and bureaucrats have tried to "solve" the problems created by one set of regulations by imposing another set, and so forth, in a vicious spiral of increased costs, rationing, suffering, and death. Just as a doctor would not attempt to treat a burn victim by exposing him to more heat, so we should not attempt to solve our health care problems through more government intervention.

The only moral and practical solution to this now-behemoth problem is to acknowledge that government intervention in health care and in health insurance is wrong, and to start in earnest to eliminate all such interference. This is the *moral* approach to solving the problem because it recognizes that the producers of health care goods and services have an inalienable right to dispose of the fruits of their thought and labor as they see fit, seeking their best interests through free trade in the marketplace. And it is the *practical* approach to solving the problem because it will lead to high-quality medical care at the prices that make such care possible—the prices on which providers and patients voluntarily agree.

A first step in the right direction would be to repeal EMTALA [Emergency Medical Treatment and Active Labor Act], allowing doctors and hospitals to decide whom they will treat and on what terms, and whether they will treat a given patient at all. As a matter of moral fact, doctors have the same rights as plumbers, accountants, grocers, and lawyers—rights that include the right to decide which patients they will treat and to refuse patients who cannot afford them.

The Sufficiency of Charity

As to the question of how those who cannot afford medical care will receive it, we must bear in mind that government is not taking care of them now and is logically incapable of ever doing so, for the simple reason that government does not and cannot produce goods or services. Insofar as people who cannot afford medical care are receiving it, the care is being provided by productive American citizens, doctors, and hospitals. And we must bear in mind that, in the words of philosopher Leonard Peikoff, Americans who cannot afford medical care "are necessarily a small minority in a free or even semi-free country. If they were the majority, the country would be an utter bankrupt and could not even think of a national medical program."

We must work toward the elimination of Medicare, Medicaid, and all other government insurance programs that allegedly benefit the aged and the poor.

Those unable to afford any particular medical services would have to rely on voluntary charity, not on the empty promises of government. Individually, Americans are the most generous people in the world, and they have always been so. For example, American individuals, corporations, and foundations gave $1.5 billion to aid victims of the December 26, 2004, Sumatra earthquake and tsunami, more than double the amount any government provided, including the United States.

Quoting Dr. Peikoff again:

And such charity, I may say, was always forthcoming in the past in America. The advocates of Medicaid and Medicare under LBJ [President Lyndon B. Johnson] did not claim that the poor or old in the '60s got bad care; they claimed that it was an affront for anyone to have to depend on charity.

But the fact is: You don't abolish charity by calling it something else. If a person is getting health care for nothing, simply because he is breathing, he is still getting charity, whether or not any politician, lobbyist or activist calls it a "right." To call it a right when the recipient did not earn it is merely to compound the evil. It is charity still—though now extorted by criminal tactics of force, while hiding under a dishonest name.

As shown, charity already abounds in America and would be even more abundant if the government removed its coercive hands from the health care and health insurance industries and consumers. Even with the government violating rights to the extent that it currently does, many examples indicate the sufficiency of charity in this regard. Here are just a few: The Shriners Hospitals [for Children] provide free care to children and adults with orthopedic, spinal cord, and burn injuries. St. Jude [Children's Research] Hospital provides free catastrophic care for children. Pharmaceutical companies provide enormous quantities of prescription drugs to those who are unable to afford them; for instance, they provided free (or nearly free) prescription drugs to about 6.2 million people in 2003 alone, and have been providing free prescription medicines to those unable to afford them for years. And there are hundreds of other examples.

The Need to Eliminate Government Interference

With sufficient cultural support, eliminating EMTALA would be easy and would cause little disruption of services. It could be phased out over the course of a year with no difficulty. By setting a definite date in the future, for example, December 31, 2008, at which EMTALA would end, everyone would have ample opportunity to learn the law, and willing doctors, hospitals, and philanthropic organizations would have time to ramp up their charity care.

We must also eliminate the preferential tax-exempt status of employer-provided health insurance. The tax code must be changed to treat all Americans equally with respect to how they purchase health insurance and medical services. The existing unjust tax provision could also be phased out over a relatively short time, perhaps two or three years. But we must begin today by recognizing that this tax law is unjust both to those without employer-sponsored insurance and to those with such insurance. It gives preferential tax treatment to those with health insurance, and it treats those same employees as helpless dependents by making it economically unsound for them to choose and pay for their own insurance plans.

Further, we must eliminate all insurance mandates—including mandatory community rating, guaranteed issue, guaranteed renewability, and benefit mandates—and we must emphatically reject any call for individual or employer mandates. Insurance companies have a moral right to offer whatever policies and terms they deem marketable. Under a free market in health care, the types of insurance plans and coverage will undoubtedly change, but such changes will be the result of insurers and consumers acting according to their best judgment—by mutual consent and in each party's best interest. That is the beauty of a truly free market. . . .

We must work toward the elimination of Medicare, Medicaid, and all other government insurance programs that allegedly benefit the aged and the poor. As we have seen, these programs provide illusory "coverage," while actually reducing or eliminating patients' access to doctors. These programs could be phased out over several years beginning with the passage of a law to the effect that no person under the age of thirty-five will pay into or receive any benefits from Medicare. This would enable those under thirty-five to begin planning for their own future, long-term medical costs and enable insurers to plan for the future as well. Likewise, we could start reducing both the extent of Medicaid benefits and the number of beneficiaries, by limiting the number of years that a person could receive Medicaid benefits, in ways similar to those methods used very effectively by the Clinton administration to reduce welfare rolls.

Finally, we must repeal HIPAA [Health Insurance Portability and Accountability Act] and all other government regulations involving health insurance or medical care. It is immoral for doctors to be subject to criminal penalties for documentation errors that violate no rights and have nothing to do with the quality of patient care. These laws do nothing but increase the amount of time spent on useless, or nearly useless, paperwork. Eliminating HIPAA and many other regulations would enable doctors to return to the practice of medicine, providing patients with more access to quality care. Again, eliminating these laws could be done easily, by setting forth a future time at which the law would expire.

One Solution

One innovative insurance solution that is likely to become commonplace in a truly free marketplace is a combination of Health Savings Accounts (HSAs) and high-deductible, low-cost catastrophic insurance. HSAs enable individuals to save money for possible future medical expenses and to spend their own money on routine health care according to their own best judgment. Catastrophic insurance provides an economical way to protect against low-probability but highly expensive accidents and serious illnesses. Economic analyses have shown that a combination of these two kinds of plans provides high-quality care at a lower cost than traditional insurance plans. The Whole Foods grocery chain, for example, has been successful in using HSAs in conjunction with high-deductible catastrophic insurance policies to cut costs, while encouraging individual responsibility and preserving quality of care. This program is extremely popular with Whole Foods employees.

Although the goal of these proposed changes—a fully free market in health care and health insurance—cannot be achieved overnight, movement in the right direction can and should begin immediately. The only moral and practical way to proceed is to recognize the proper end and to consciously and consistently move toward that end by taking whatever steps in that direction . . . at any given time. What we must *not* do is shy away from recognizing and proclaiming the proper goal—the complete eradication of every trace of government interference in medicine and health insurance—or the fundamental moral justification for pursuing that goal: the individual's moral right to his life, liberty, and property.

The Free Market

Only the ideal of the free market—based on the principle of individual rights—provides a solid foundation for genuine and practical reform. And only a free market in medicine can deliver the properly (i.e., voluntarily) priced high-quality health care that Americans deserve. This last point is evident in the sectors of medicine with the least government regulation, such as cosmetic surgery and LASIK eye surgery. The clear pattern in these sectors is a continual decrease in prices and improvement in quality. As health economist Devon Herrick stated in testimony before the U.S. Congress:

> [D]espite a marked increase in demand between 1992 and the present, cosmetic surgeons' fees remained relatively stable. The average increase in prices for medical services from 1992 through 2005 was 77 percent. The increase in the price of all goods, as measured by the consumer price index (CPI), was 39 percent. Cosmetic surgery prices only went up about 22 percent. Thus, while the price of medical services generally rose almost twice as fast as the CPI, the price of cosmetic surgery went up slightly more than half as much. Put another way, while the real price of health care paid for by third parties rose, the real price of self-pay medicine fell. Another example of price competition is the market for corrective eye surgery. In 1999, only a few years after LASIK was approved, the price was about $2,100 per eye, according to the ophthalmic market research firm MarketScope. Within a short time, competition drove the price down to slightly

more than $1,600. The cost per eye of the standard LASIK is now about 20 percent lower than six years earlier. Competition held prices in check until a new innovation arrived for which patients were willing to pay more. By 2003, surgeons began to perform a newer, more-advanced custom wavefront-guided LASIK procedure.

In other words, the market can and does bring down health care costs while improving services when allowed to operate without government interference.

The market can and does bring down health care costs while improving services when allowed to operate without government interference.

A free market in health insurance and health care works because it recognizes that health care is a commodity produced by individuals who have a right to offer that commodity for trade on whatever terms they see fit—and that consumers have the right to accept or reject those terms as they see fit. When all parties are free to trade voluntarily, according to their own best judgment, the result is lower costs and higher quality—a fact that is evident throughout the economy and recognized by all reputable economists.

The relatively free American marketplace has done a magnificent job in providing other necessities of life such as food, shelter, and clothing; it can do the same for health care and health insurance—if we free up these markets.

In a truly free market, other creative and innovative solutions will arise—solutions that have not yet been conceived by any politician, policy analyst, or by the authors of this [viewpoint]. The fact that we cannot foresee all the possible good ideas is not an undesirable "bug" of the free market, but rather one of its marvelous features. Just as someone twenty years ago could not have imagined the specific innovations and benefits that would arise from a free market in the then-fledgling Internet industry (consider eBay, Amazon.com, Google, iPhones, etc.), so people today cannot imagine the specific innovations and benefits that would arise from a free market in medicine and health insurance. What is certain is that the freer the market, the more innovation and benefits will arise.

Health Care Is a Right, Not a Privilege

Bernie Sanders

Bernie Sanders is a U.S. senator from Vermont. Sanders is the first member of the Senate to identify as a socialist, although he does not belong to a formal political party.

L et's be clear. Our health care system is disintegrating. Today, 46 million people have no health insurance and even more are underinsured with high deductibles and co-payments. At a time when 60 million people, including many with insurance, do not have access to a medical home, more than 18,000 Americans die every year from preventable illnesses because they do not get to the doctor when they should. This is six times the number who died at the tragedy of 9/11 [2001 terrorist attacks on the United States]—but this occurs every year.

The State of U.S. Health Care

In the midst of this horrendous lack of coverage, the U.S. spends far more per capita on health care than any other nation—and health care costs continue to soar. At $2.4 trillion dollars, and 18 percent of our GDP [gross domestic product], the skyrocketing cost of health care in this country is unsustainable both from a personal and macroeconomic perspective.

At the individual level, the average American spends about $7,900 per year on health care. Despite that huge outlay, a recent study found that medical problems contributed to 62

Bernie Sanders, "Health Care Is a Right, Not a Privilege," *Huffington Post*, June 8, 2009. Reproduced by permission of the author.

percent of all bankruptcies in 2007. From a business perspective, General Motors spends more on health care per automobile than on steel while small business owners are forced to divert hard-earned profits into health coverage for their employees—rather than new business investments. And, because of rising costs, many businesses are cutting back drastically on their level of health care coverage or are doing away with it entirely.

Further, despite the fact that we spend almost twice as much per person on health care as any other country, our health care outcomes lag behind many other nations. We get poor value for what we spend. According to the World Health Organization, the United States ranks 37th in terms of health system performance and we are far behind many other countries in terms of such important indices as infant mortality, life expectancy and preventable deaths.

As the health care debate heats up in Washington[, D.C.], we as a nation have to answer two very fundamental questions. First, should all Americans be entitled to health care as a right and not a privilege—which is the way every other major country treats health care and the way we respond to such other basic needs as education, police and fire protection? Second, if we are to provide quality health care to all, how do we accomplish that in the most cost-effective way possible?

I think the answer to the first question is pretty clear, and one of the reasons that Barack Obama was elected president. Most Americans do believe that all of us should have health care coverage, and that nobody should be left out of the system. The real debate is how we accomplish that goal in an affordable and sustainable way. In that regard, I think the evidence is overwhelming that we must end the private insurance company domination of health care in our country and move toward a publicly funded, single-payer Medicare for All approach.

The Waste in the Current System

Our current private health insurance system is the most costly, wasteful, complicated and bureaucratic in the world. Its function is not to provide quality health care for all, but to make huge profits for those who own the companies. With thousands of different health benefit programs designed to maximize profits, private health insurance companies spend an incredible (30 percent) of each health care dollar on administration and billing, exorbitant CEO [chief executive officer] compensation packages, advertising, lobbying and campaign contributions. Public programs like Medicare, Medicaid and the VA [Veterans Affairs] are administered for far less.

Most Americans do believe that all of us should have health care coverage, and that nobody should be left out of the system.

In recent years, while we have experienced an acute shortage of primary health care doctors as well as nurses and dentists, we are paying for a huge increase in health care bureaucrats and bill collectors. Over the last three decades, the number of administrative personnel has grown by 25 times the number of physicians. Not surprisingly, while health care costs are soaring, so are the profits of private health insurance companies. From 2003 to 2007, the combined profits of the nation's major health insurance companies increased by 170 percent. And, while more and more Americans are losing their jobs and health insurance, the top executives in the industry are receiving lavish compensation packages. It's not just William McGuire, the former head of UnitedHealth, who several years ago accumulated stock options worth an estimated $1.6 billion, or CIGNA CEO [H.] Edward Hanway who made more than $120 million in the last five years. The reality is that CEO compensation for the top seven health insurance companies now averages $14.2 million.

Moving toward a national health insurance program that provides cost-effective, universal, comprehensive and quality health care for all will not be easy. The powerful special interests—the insurance companies, drug companies and medical equipment suppliers—will wage an all-out fight to make sure that we maintain the current system that enables them to make billions of dollars. In recent years they have spent hundreds of millions on lobbying, campaign contributions and advertising and, with unlimited resources, they will continue spending as much as they need.

But, at the end of the day, as difficult as it may be, the fight for a national health care program will prevail. Like the civil rights movement, the struggle for women's rights and other grassroots efforts, justice in this country is often delayed—but it will not be denied. We shall overcome!

CHAPTER2

What Ethics
Should Guide
Organ Transplants?

Overview: Organ Transplantation

The Gift of a Lifetime

The Gift of a Lifetime is a Web site—a production of Fusion-spark Media—that contains information about organ and tissue transplantation in America.

In the United States, more than 84,000 men, women and children are waiting for organ transplants. Their struggle to live depends on a complex and technologically advanced organ allocation system that links patients with organs donated by strangers.

Subjected to intense scrutiny by the federal government, the public, and the medical profession, no other aspect of modern medicine is more analyzed and debated. Such scrutiny is essential. Organ transplantation is built upon altruism and public trust. If anything shakes that trust, then everyone loses.

The Organ Waiting List

In 1984, the National Organ Transplant Act established the Organ Procurement and Transplantation Network (OPTN), a national organ-sharing system to guarantee, among other things, fairness in the allocation of organs for transplant. Since 1984, the nonprofit United Network for Organ Sharing (UNOS) located in Richmond, Virginia, has operated the OPTN, under a contract with the Division of Transplantation in the Department of Health and Human Services. UNOS maintains a central computer network containing the names of all patients waiting for kidney, heart, liver, lung, intestine, pancreas and multiple-organ transplants; the UNOS "Organ

The Gift of a Lifetime, "Understanding Donation: The Organ Transplant Waiting List," Accessed January 4, 2009. www.organtransplants.org. Reproduced by permission.

Center" is staffed 24 hours a day to respond to requests to list patients, change status of patients, and help coordinate the placement of organs.

Organ transplantation is built upon altruism and public trust.

Patients on the waiting list are in end-stage organ failure and have been evaluated by a transplant physician at hospitals in the U.S. where organ transplants are performed. Policies that dictate organ allocation are created and revised through a consensus-building process that involves UNOS committees and a board of directors, all composed of transplant physicians, government officials, specialists in immunology and experts in organ donation, as well as donor families, transplant recipients and members of the general public. Any proposed changes to the organ allocation rules are openly debated and published for public comment before being implemented.

Principles Guiding Organ Allocation

Specifics of waiting list rules, which can be seen at the OPTN Web site, vary by organ. General principles, such as a patient's medical urgency, blood, tissue and size match with the donor, time on the waiting list and proximity to the donor, guide the distribution of organs. Under certain circumstances, special allowances are made for children. For example, children under age 11 who need kidneys are automatically assigned additional points. Factors such as a patient's income, celebrity status, and race or ethnic background play no role in determining allocation of organs.

Contrary to popular belief, waiting on the list for a transplant is not like taking a number at the deli counter and waiting for your turn to order. In some respects, even the word "list" is misleading; the list is really a giant pool of patients. There is no ranking or patient order until there is a donor, because each donor's blood type, size and genetic characteristics are different. Therefore, when a donor is entered into the national computer system, the patients that match that donor, and therefore the "list," are different each time.

The other major guiding principle in organ allocation is: local patients first. The country is divided into 11 geographic regions, each served by a federally designated organ procurement organization (OPO), which is responsible for coordinating all organ donations. With the exception of perfectly matched kidneys and the most urgent liver patients, first priority goes to patients at transplant hospitals located in the region served by the OPO. Next in priority are patients in areas served by nearby OPOs; and finally, only if no patients in these communities can use the organ, it is offered to patients elsewhere in the U.S.

Such locally oriented allocation makes medical sense because less time between donor and recipient usually means more chance of a successful transplant as well as fewer logistical complications that could threaten the viability of the organ. Experience has shown, furthermore, that people are more likely to donate organs if they know that other people in their own community will benefit.

Thus, contrary to the image of organs always crisscrossing the country, 80 percent of all organs are donated and used, in the same geographic area.

Debates About Organ Allocation

Of course, debates about organ allocation will continue as long as there is such a large gap between patients who need transplants and the number of organs donated. Who, for example, should get priority, people who are the sickest or those who have the greatest chance of surviving and achieving a long life? And what is the significance, if any, of someone's personal behavior? Should a much-needed heart go to a person who was a heavy smoker or a liver to someone who has suffered from alcoholism? These are difficult questions for which there are no easy answers.

The National Organ Transplant Act of 1984 also created the Scientific Registry of Transplant Recipients, which is now maintained at the University of Michigan, also under contract to the Division of Transplantation. Through the Scientific Registry, patients can obtain hospital-specific information about transplant survival rates as well as the performance of regional OPOs. Because this registry extends back more than twenty years and has detailed records of treatments and outcomes for more than 200,000 organ recipients, transplantation is by far the best-documented aspect of modern medicine.

The Sale of Kidneys for Transplantation Is Ethical

Cord Jefferson

Cord Jefferson is a writer who lives in New York.

On Wednesday night [April 1, 2009], Natalie Cole announced on *Larry King Live* that both of her kidneys were failing following a decades-long battle with hepatitis C; without a kidney transplant, she lamented, she'd be looking at a life of dialysis.

Within minutes of her sharing her illness with the world, dozens of Cole's fans had e-mailed the show with offers of their organs. "There are some great human beings out there," Cole said of the outpouring. It's a heartwarming story, but it also underscores a major problem in America: the giant gulf between those in need of an organ and those willing to donate one. When patients waiting in an endless line for a kidney transplant are relegated to making on-air pleas for help, something's seriously wrong with the system.

Cash for Kidneys

As Americans everywhere wait to see how Barack Obama will handle medical care, allow me to suggest to the new president a solution: an open, regulated, and legal cash-for-kidneys market in the United States.

It's a subject very near to my abdomen. Last summer, I traveled to Riyadh, Saudi Arabia, to donate a kidney to my ailing father, who lives and works there. By the time I arrived, his kidneys were functioning at 5 percent of their capacity and he was going to four hours of dialysis, three times a week. After the sessions, I would watch him struggle up the stairs, his

Cord Jefferson, "Let Natalie Cole Buy a Kidney," *Daily Beast*, April 3, 2009. Reproduced by permission.

weary body shaking, belying my childhood memories of riding on his broad, solid shoulders. Giving him my left kidney was an honor, and I'd do it again—even if there weren't thousands of dollars in it for me the next time.

When patients waiting in an endless line for a kidney transplant are relegated to making on-air pleas for help, something's seriously wrong with the system.

See, like many in the creative underclass of New York, I was gainfully employed, yet still without health insurance. When my father's illness got gradually worse, I eagerly volunteered to donate. But because kidney donation in America is a nonprofit enterprise, the myriad expenses associated with the operation and the years of aftercare fell beyond my ability to pay. Before I could even broach this dilemma with my dad, he wired me thousands of dollars to pay for insurance and initial testing. Would I have gone through with the donation without the money? Probably—only because he was my father. The point is that the offer of money made me absolutely certain I wanted to donate.

To make such a sacrifice for a stranger, I'd almost definitely require some similar monetary encouragement. And with 83,000 Americans desperately waiting at least five years for a donated kidney—thousands of whom will die before they get it—the U.S. government has a responsibility to provide that encouragement.

Because although one can live without two kidneys, the process of extracting one is hell. Before the operation, when I wasn't in the hospital giving blood or getting weighed, I was at home, collecting my urine in a big plastic bottle for testing. After the surgery, I would sleep half the day away, partly because I was on heavy medication and partly because it hurt to be awake. Sneezing and laughing were agony; simple things like rolling over in bed required yoga training. Even six months later, my surgeon told me not to jog or play tennis. I'm completely fine now, but the fact remains that unless you're Natalie Cole, it would probably be next to impossible to get a stranger to make such a sacrifice for nothing more than good karma.

The Kidney Market Outside
the United States

Were the U.S. to create a cash-for-kidneys market, we wouldn't be the first. Currently the only nation in the world that allows the buying and selling of living donors' organs is Iran, which adopted the practice in 1988 when it could no longer ignore the rate at which patients with end-stage renal disease were outpacing willing kidney donors. Whatever you might think of Iran's politics, the results have been noteworthy. According to an article published in the *Clinical Journal of the American Society of Nephrology* in 2006, in the years since Iran started the nationally regulated and funded program, the wait for a renal transplant has vanished. In Iran, the kidney waits for you.

Outside of Iran, the only place to easily obtain a kidney is on the thriving black market, an option my father says he also considered, and one that's just a Google search away. The World Health Organization estimates that around 14,000 kidney transplants per year—some of them performed right here in America—are done with illegally obtained organs, kidneys purchased from living Indians, Pakistanis, Brazilians, often for about $5,000.

I asked my dad if his thoughts of purchasing an organ from the third world were ever accompanied by pangs of guilt. "Absolutely none!" he said. "The arrogance of those who decide that they know what is best for me, you, the poor, and the sick is just staggering."

Countries less offensive to Americans than Iran are also considering legalization. Last week, Singapore's parliament legalized monetary reimbursement for living organ donors. It's now completely aboveboard—and probably expected—for a kidney recipient in Singapore to pay for his donor's travel expenses, lodging, or time off from work. The hope is that the legislation will lead to a larger, government-run version of America's National Transplant Assistance Fund, a nonprofit that provides some assistance for some uninsured organ donors' medical expenses (though it's far too small to help everyone in need, and doesn't offer any cash "reward" on top of expenses as incentive for potential donors).

Every day, 17 Americans die while waiting for a kidney.

Critics of the Organ Trade

The chief argument against a cash-for-kidneys system is that it will summon an outright organ market, one in which the rich procure second chances at life from the poor. Nancy Scheper-Hughes, a professor of anthropology at [University of California,] Berkeley and one of America's most vocal critics of the organ trade, criticizes kidney sales for two main reasons. What she most takes issue with is that organ sellers are often impoverished laborers who return from their surgeries unable to work and without the proper aftercare. Soon, their fee is spent on things other than their health, and they're drinking unclean water and eating bad food, neglecting a body that needs time to recover. The professor's second point is less tangible: She believes it's dangerous to commodify the human body. "It's the sense that body and soul are connected," she once told the *Christian Science Monitor*, "and selling your body is chipping away at what gives you existence."

Her first argument doesn't hold water. Every reputable proponent of legalized organ sales (which, by the way, includes both Dr. Arthur Matas, former president of the American Society of Transplant Surgeons, and Dr. Benjamin Hippen, transplant nephrologist at the Carolinas Medical Center) says they envision a market that's strictly regulated by government bodies, preventing donors from getting hustled and left to fall ill. As it stands now, the criminality of the organ trade is what's dangerous. My father recalled asking his surgeons if buying a kidney in the black market was safe. "They couldn't give me an answer because there are no records kept in the black market," he said. "But what they could do was tell me about all the people they saw who were now sick and dying because the black market is unregulated."

Dr. Michael Friedlaender, head of the kidney transplant follow-up unit at Hadassah Medical Center in Jerusalem, has likened the black market organ trade to abortions in years past: "Though I hate to compare it, because this saves lives, it's like abortions, where the illegal state of abortion caused terrible things to happen to young women," he says. "[With organs], we have no control over standards, over payments, over follow-up health care. You can make standards only for things that are legal."

As for Scheper-Hughes' point about commodifying the body, since when is that new? There are countless instances in which America allows the poor to do dangerous things with their bodies for money. Working-class people shoulder the burden of war; they risk their lungs and limbs in mine shafts, factories, slaughterhouses, and fishing boats. And it remains perfectly legal for a surrogate mother to sell her womb—also no small physical burden. What makes a kidney so special?

I think it's similar to America's failure to consider legalizing marijuana. Both are supported by many medical professionals, but the political will to change the law exists for neither. Yet every day, 17 Americans die while waiting for a kidney. It's an organ most of us could give to them easily, if only there were a system in place to compensate us for our trouble. My father was lucky to have my support and the resources to go elsewhere if he didn't. But with such a definite source of life constantly operating just out of reach, it's a shame that luck comes into the equation at all.

Charity, Not Money, Should Guide Kidney Transplantation

Gerald D. Coleman

Gerald D. Coleman is the vice president for corporate ethics for the Daughters of Charity Health System and a lecturer in moral theology at Santa Clara University.

The Organ Procurement and Transplantation Network estimates that there are currently more than 89,000 potential organ candidates on waiting lists. In the past decade, the number of persons nationwide waiting for kidneys has more than doubled to at least 65,500 and could reach 100,000 by 2010. This growing number is being driven by older patients between 50 and 65 years old. Depending on geographic location, the average wait is from three to nine years.

The United Network for Organ Sharing (UNOS), which oversees transplantation for the federal government, calculates that every day 17 people die while waiting for a vital organ. Living kidney donations represent 94 percent of all living donations. Organ donation between living persons has now surpassed that of donations from deceased persons; adults account for 95 percent of transplants using kidneys from cadavers.

Allocation of a Scarce Resource

Two recent cases highlight significant concerns.

While riding his Harley-Davidson motorcycle in 2002, 30-year-old Shawn Stringfellow drove off an interstate highway near Denver, Colo., and struck a construction barrel. The next day he was declared brain dead, while life support kept his heart beating. With his family's consent, calls went out to transplant centers that Stringfellow's two kidneys were available.

Clois Guthrie, an 85-year-old patient, was third on the regional organ waiting list for a kidney transplant. In light of his overall health condition, he likely had only a few more years to live. Two younger candidates were first and second on the list. One nephrologist on the transplant team argued that the kidneys could last decades if given to a younger patient. Another team member claimed that it is unethical to give a young kidney to an 85-year-old patient. Guthrie was then removed from the waiting list.

The allocation of a scarce resource is a moral issue. UNOS already has given patients younger than 18 an advantage by moving them to the front of the line for high-quality organs from donors younger than 35. In 2007 the U.S. Health Resources and Services Administration is expected to consider a national policy on the allocation of available organs for transplantation. While patients older than 79 would no longer be accepted, patients 70 to 79 would be considered for subpar organs from living donors, usually relatives.

The allocation of a scarce resource is a moral issue.

From a Stranger to a Friend

In another case, Herbert Davis, a 65-year-old physicist from Menlo Park, Calif., needed a new kidney. He had lived with damaged kidneys for decades as a result of a childhood infection. After four years of dialysis, he received his first kidney transplant in 1995. This transplanted kidney failed nine years later. His wife was not a compatible kidney match and sent an emotional letter to 140 friends and relatives pleading for a donation. One of them knew Matt Thompson.

Matt Thompson read the letter and felt that the plea was addressed to him. "I felt that God was compelling me to help out," he said. Thompson is a born-again Christian and has done missionary work in Brazil. He is married and has an infant daughter. Davis and Thompson had never met nor did they know each other. When Thompson contacted Davis's transplant program, he was turned down flat. He was not permitted to donate an organ to a stranger because of the medical risks involved. This is a regulation in many U.S. transplantation programs. Hospitals also worry that a donation from a stranger may involve undisclosed financial incentives.

Davis and Thompson then forged a friendship around the kidney transplant, however, and the situation changed. The hospital relented. "We started off as strangers, we moved to friends, and after the surgery, we're now a family," Thompson explained. The surgery successfully took place on November 14, 2006, at the University of California, San Francisco Medical Center.

The "Do No Harm" Principle

In this case, the moral issue was rooted in medicine's "do no harm" principle that requires physicians to justify performing risky surgery on a healthy donor. Noted bioethicist Arthur Caplan has explained that principle: "The closer the relationship, the more medicine feels comfortable saying, 'We'll subject you to risk.'" He argues that there is a scientific consensus that "ethically, you don't force relationships."

Dr. John Scandling, medical director of the adult kidney and pancreas transplant program at Stanford University, stresses the risk involved: "It's major surgery. You can die." Stanford bioethicist David Magnus adds that the process whereby Herbert Davis attained the kidney donated by Matt Thompson is "inappropriate, absolutely." Says Magnus, "Living donor programs aren't intended to find ways for people to artificially become friends, but to allow people who are close friends to donate." He characterized the Davis-Thompson arrangement as "just a way of skirting the system." Stanford restricts organ donations to friends and family.

At California Pacific Medical Center, surgeons evaluate "relationship" on a case-by-case basis using the criterion that "there is no sliding scale of friendship." It is critical to ensure that donors have the right motives and are not being coerced. At the University of California, Davis transplant program, strangers are allowed to donate but must do so anonymously for the patients most in need.

Ethical Concerns

These two cases raise significant ethical issues. Should the presumption for an organ transplant be that younger people are always to be preferred since organs are too often squandered on the old? And should donors be limited to family or close friends?

While organ or tissue transplantation from a dead to a living person presents no moral problem in itself, four other issues are relevant: the expense involved in the medical procedure, assurance of the total brain death of the donor, attaining proper consent and assuring the appropriate separation between the physicians who make the donation medically possible and those who belong to and participate in the transplantation team. This avoids a conflict of interest—for example, if a doctor were on the transplant team and at the same time were the patient's doctor, he/she could hasten death to make the organ more quickly available.

The Catholic Tradition

Before 1950, Catholic moralists argued that living organ transplantation was unethical because it necessarily involved harming and injuring a person's body. The principle of totality forbids mutilation. In 1956, Gerald Kelly, S.J., suggested a different way of viewing organ donations when he wrote that "by a sort of instinctive judgment . . . the giving of a part of one's body to help a sick man is not only morally justifiable, but, in some instances, actually heroic." He limited his moral reasoning justifying organ transplantation to "the principle of fraternal love or charity," provided that there was only limited harm to the donor.

Father Kelly and later Catholic moralists distinguished between anatomical integrity and functional integrity. Anatomical integrity refers to the physical integrity of the human body and functional integrity refers to its efficiency. If a person were missing a kidney, for example, there would be a lack of anatomical integrity, but there is functional integrity since one healthy kidney provides efficiency.

These moral judgments for both living and deceased organ donations found their way into papal approval.

- In 1995, John Paul II declared in his encyclical *The Gospel of Life* that our daily life "should be filled with self-giving love for others. A particularly praiseworthy example is the donation of organs, performed in an ethically acceptable manner, with a view to offering a chance of health and even of life itself to the sick who sometimes have no other hope" (no. 86).

- In an "Address to the International Congress on [Organ] Transplants," in 2000, the pope described the practice of organ donation as "a genuine act of love."

- *The Catechism of the Catholic Church* (1992) identifies organ donation as a concrete sign of solidarity with other members of the human community (no. 2301).

- *Ethical and Religious Directives for Catholic Health Care Services* (2001) notes that "Catholic health care institutions should encourage and provide the means whereby those who wish to do so may arrange for the donation of their organs and bodily tissue" (no. 63).

The Sale of Organs

In light of this Catholic tradition, the two cases summarized [in this viewpoint] suggest certain challenges and guidelines. Since there will always be a shortage of suitable organs and tissues for transplant, the current system of obtaining organs and allotting them must be more carefully defined. The overall health benefit to the candidate needs to be a significant factor in allotments.

Before 1950, Catholic moralists argued that living organ transplantation was unethical because it necessarily involved harming and injuring a person's body.

Charity and human solidarity must be the motivating factors that justify organ transplantation. While the sale of organs by living donors is common practice in some countries, it is always unethical and should be made illegal. Human solidarity must be considered when evaluating the relationship between the candidate and the donor.

The Internet has vastly expanded opportunities to link donors with patients by way of e-mail pleas or urgent postings on Craigslist.org or other sites (like www.matchingdonors .com). Behind the sale of organs is the poverty of the individual willing to sell, not to mention the financial interest of any middlemen involved in transacting the sale. Organ transplantation for sale, however, is ethically wrong. In the United States it is illegal to receive payment for a donated organ. A "free market" for the buying and selling of organs radically subverts the basic motives of charity and human solidarity.

Ethical Guidelines for Organ Transplantation

Total brain death must be maintained as a criterion before organ transplantation is ethical. In the case of an anencephalic [an absence of most or all of the brain] infant, for instance, it is not permissible to remove organs because the child's cerebral cortex has not developed. Yet the absence of the higher brain does not alone constitute death. At the same time, it is permissible to place an adult or infant on a respirator to ensure that blood will continue permeating the organs so that they could be suitable for transplant after clinical signs have certified that total brain death has occurred.

While the sale of organs by living donors is common practice in some countries, it is always unethical and should be made illegal.

In sum, the following ethical norms should inform organ transplantations:

1. A patient's general health condition and age should be a consideration.

2. Unless the donation is anonymous, some level of authentic connection must be present between the donor and the patient.

3. Such a level of connection establishes a reason to justify proportionately the risk to the donor.

4. The functional integrity of a donor must never be impaired, even though the donor's anatomical integrity is compromised.

5. Stewardship of one's body demands that we have a serious reason for harming the health and anatomical integrity of our body.

6. Fraternal love must justify all organ transplantations. This principle negates any monetary gain. Selling one's organs is intrinsically reprehensible. "Cash for flesh" must never be tolerated.

7. The donor's consent must be fully informed and freely given.

Individuals Should Become Organ Donors to Stop Organ Sales

William Saletan

William Saletan is Slate's *national correspondent and the author of* Bearing Right: How Conservatives Won the Abortion War.

If you lose your job, you can sell your home. If you lose your home, you can sell your possessions. If you lose your possessions, you can prostitute yourself. And if you lose everything else, you can sell one more thing: your organs.

The Global Organ Market

Twice in the last two weeks [March 26–April 6, 2007], transplant experts from around the world have convened in Europe to discuss the emerging global market in human flesh. Two maps presented at the meetings tell the story. One shows countries from which patients have traveled for organs in the last three years: Saudi Arabia, Taiwan, Malaysia, South Korea. The other shows countries from which organs have been sold: China, Pakistan, Colombia, the Philippines.

The numbers on the maps add up to thousands. According to the World Health Organization, the annual tally of international kidney transactions alone is about 6,000. The evidence includes reports from brokers and physicians, accounts from Indian villages, surveys of hospitals in Japan, government records in Singapore, and scars in Egyptian slums. In Pakistan, 40 percent of people in some villages are turning up with only one kidney. Charts presented at the meetings show the number of "donations" from unrelated Pakistanis skyrocketing. Two-thirds of the people getting these organs are foreigners. Data from the Philippines show the same thing.

The Demand for Organs

The first successful organ transplant took place half a century ago. Since then, diabetes, hypertension, and other kidney-destroying diseases have spread. Antibiotics have improved, as have drugs that suppress the immune response to foreign organs. More people need transplants, and more can be saved by them. But donations haven't kept up with demand. An estimated 170,000 patients in the U.S. and Europe are on waiting lists. More than 70,000 Americans are waiting for kidneys, and the list has grown at a rate of almost 5,000 per year. People are dying.

Instead of waiting, many patients have set out to recruit their own donors. They started with billboards, then moved to Web sites such as MatchingDonors.com, JoeNeedsaLiver.com, and HelpMyGrandpa.com. Around the world, people have learned that their organs are assets. Peruvians, Ukrainians, Chinese hospitals, and American inmates advertise their innards. Last year, a South Korean playwright used his kidney as collateral for a loan.

Politicians have tried to rein in this market. The United States banned organ sales two decades ago. India did the same in 1994, and China followed last year. But when lives are at stake, rules get bent. To procure more organs, doctors have discarded brain-death standards, donor age limits, and recipient health requirements. States have let transplant agencies put patients on life support, contrary to their living wills, to preserve their organs. If Congress revises its ban on organ sales, as some advocates hope, lawmakers in South Carolina plan to offer prisoners reduced jail time in exchange for organs or marrow.

International Organ Commerce

If national governments can't control wages or prices in a global economy, they certainly can't control the purchase of extended life. In the last two years, Israeli organ brokers shifted their business from Colombia to China for faster service. If China closes its doors, they can shift again. In Pakistan, kidneys already sell for a fraction of what Chinese hospitals charged. Brokers can compare organ prices from country to country, just like wheat or corn.

Around the world, people have learned that their organs are assets.

Already, bans on organ commerce are crumbling. Indians who lost their livelihoods in the tsunami of 2004 sold their kidneys, ignoring the law. Bulgaria imposes stiff sentences on organ traders, but that didn't deter a local hospital from serving Israeli transplant tourists last year. Nor did China's ban stop a Chinese hospital from offering a liver to a BBC correspondent. Three weeks ago, a Korean newspaper reported that China's organ crackdown had simply raised the price of a Chinese kidney in South Korea.

Some reformers think they can solve the organ shortage and tame the market by legalizing sales. Their latest proposal, presented at one of the European meetings last week by Dr. Arthur Matas of the University of Minnesota, is a single-payer system for organs. It's half libertarian and half socialist. On the one hand, Matas says markets for eggs and sperm are harmless, kidney purchases can save countries money, and offering poor people cash for organs is no more coercive than offering them money to work in mines or join the army. On the other hand, he thinks the government can fix kidney prices and determine who gets them.

Good luck. As any country with national health insurance knows, people find ways to buy more than they're allotted.

Ration medical care abroad, and affluent foreigners will come here. Ration organs here, and affluent Americans will go abroad, as they're already doing. It's true that payments would elicit more "donations." But studies reviewed at the meetings in Europe show that flooding the market with purchased organs reduces the incentive to donate.

Ending Sales by Ending Scarcity

The key to reversing the organ market is to turn that equation on its head. Stop fighting capitalism, and start using it. What's driving the market is scarcity. Americans, Britons, Israelis, Japanese, and South Koreans are going abroad for organs mostly because too few of their countrymen have agreed to donate organs when they die. Some have religious objections. Others are squeamish. Many figure that if they don't supply the organs, somebody else will.

If the dying can't get organs from the dead, they'll buy them from the living.

They're right. Somebody else will supply the organs. But that somebody won't be a corpse. He'll be a fisherman or an out-of-work laborer who needs cash and can't find another way to get it. The middlemen will open him up, take his kidney, pay him a fraction of the proceeds, and abandon him, because follow-up care is just another expense. If he recovers well enough to keep working, he'll be lucky.

The surest way to stop him from selling his kidney is to make it worthless, by flooding the market with free organs. If you haven't filled out a donor card, do it now. Because if the dying can't get organs from the dead, they'll buy them from the living.

A System of Presumed Consent Is Not a Good Way to Increase Available Organs

Gilbert Meilaender

Gilbert Meilaender is the Richard and Phyllis Duesenberg Professor of Christian Ethics at Valparaiso University, was a member of the President's Council on Bioethics under the George W. Bush administration, and is the author of Bioethics: A Primer for Christians.

In *The Patient as Person*, published almost forty years ago, when transplantation technology was still in its early stages, [Christian ethicist] Paul Ramsey considered different ways of procuring organs for transplant. One might invite people to "opt in," to donate organs to be used after their death (or, in the case of a paired organ such as the kidney, even before death). One might require people to "opt out" if they did not wish to have their organs taken after death for transplant, presuming consent unless they (while living) or their next of kin (after their death) specifically declined to consent. Or one might establish some kind of system whereby organs needed for transplant could be bought and sold (though he was thinking only of cadaver organs).

Opting In or Opting Out

The third of these possibilities should, Ramsey believed, be rejected altogether. But his verdict with respect to the first two was more nuanced, a comparison of their relative merits and demerits. "If giving is better than routinely taking organs to prolong the lives of patients needing transplants, then it must

Gilbert Meilaender, "The Giving and Taking of Organs," *First Things: A Monthly Journal of Religion and Public Life,* vol. 181, March 2008, pp. 14–15. Copyright © 2008 Institute on Religion and Public Life. All rights reserved. Reproduced by permission.

also be said that routinely taking them in hospital practice would be better than for us to make medical progress and extend treatment to patients by means of buying and selling cadaver organs. That society is a better and more civilized one, I have said, in which men join together in a consensual community to effect these purposes, than a society in which lives are saved routinely, without the positive consent and will of all concerned to do so. It must also be said, however, that a society would be better and more civilized in which men are joined together routinely in making cadaver organs available to prolong the lives of others than one in which this is done ostensibly by consent to the 'gift' but actually for the monetary gain of the 'donor.'"

I recalled this passage when reading of the recent proposal by Gordon Brown, prime minister of Great Britain, to deal with what he called "an avoidable human tragedy" by encouraging more people to "donate" organs. Britain's National Health Service, Brown suggested on January 14, 2008, should move to a system in which organs of the deceased would be taken for transplant, with their consent presumed, unless before death they had opted out or, after death, their family members objected to such use of their organs.

Not an Issue of Property

Ramsey's comparative analysis might remind us that the prime minister's proposal is not the worst we can envision. Ours is a world in which an increasing number of voices support some form of payment for organs (or, sometimes, for organs from specific populations, such as prisoners nearing death)—thereby turning potential donors into vendors and the body into a collection of parts that are available and alienable if the price is right. This would, Ramsey seemed to think, and I am inclined to agree, be worse than what Mr. Brown has in mind.

Nor, I think, will it do to object to Mr. Brown's proposal on the ground that my body is my property alone, no part of which should be taken or used without my explicit consent. There are, after all, occasions—if, for example, an autopsy is deemed necessary—when we allow the needs of the larger society to override the bodily integrity of a deceased individual. More important, though, is that "property" does not seem to be the right way to think of my body's relation to me. Thinking in those terms may, in fact, leave us defenseless in the face of arguments supporting a market in organs.

Nor is the body of the deceased best thought of as property of his surviving family. If their wishes about its disposal ought to be honored, that is not because they own the body. It is because the life they shared with this one who has died obligates them to give his body proper burial—and the rest of us should do nothing that makes their duty more onerous than it of necessity is or that forces them, while grieving, to fight for the right to carry out such a fundamental human duty. "There is," as William F. May once put it, "a tinge of the inhuman in the humanitarianism of those who believe that the perception of social need easily overrides all other considerations."

The Meaning of Donation

Still, there are good reasons to draw back from procuring organs for transplant by means of an opt-out system. We need an Orwell [referring to English novelist George Orwell, known for his criticism of government control] among us to note how strained the language of those, like Mr. Brown, becomes when they describe what they have in mind. His aim, he wrote, is "a different consent system" that would "increase donation levels" significantly. But, of course, it is not really "donation" that he has in mind. It is taking, not giving—and a consent that must be presumed is one that only the articulate and the powerful are likely to avoid giving. Those from whom the organs are taken, whose consent is presumed, might better be thought of as useful resources than as donors. Moreover, it would place a special burden on some groups whose beliefs—often, religious beliefs—lead them (except in special circumstances) to object to the giving or taking of bodily organs after death.

"Property" does not seem to be the right way to think of my body's relation to me.

The prime minister's language—of "an avoidable human tragedy" that could be averted were more organs available for transplant—is the sort of talk that has come to characterize most discussions of transplantation, and it begs for careful examination. It is the sort of language that can be used to justify almost anything that promises to help avoid the tragedy of death. And this is exactly the sort of language that, we have come to see, has often distorted the practice of medicine, teaching us to suppose that anything that can be done to ward off death must be done. But the deeper moral truth is that how we live, not how long, is what matters most. And among the possible "tragedies" with which we must reckon would be to live longer by means that debase or undermine our humanity.

Giving and Taking

Why is giving of organs better than taking, even if taking may provide a greater supply for transplant? To look on potential "donors" chiefly as handy collections of spare parts to be used by others is to lose the sense of the embodied human person as one who, because made finally for God, transcends every location in space and time. A person does not belong, to the whole extent of his being, to any earthly community.

Even the deceased person does not. Why, for example, did an al-Qaeda-led group in Iraq release footage of two corpses that it said were those of U.S. soldiers killed in June 2006? The video showed a decapitated body and several dead bodies being stepped on. This dishonoring of the corpses could have no point were not even the dead body still a reminder of the presence of the person, who can be the "property" of none of us, not merely a "resource" to be used for our purposes, however important they may be.

To see this, however, is to begin to see the deepest truth of all: Even the giving of organs for transplant is not unproblematic. If we first see how troubling even the giving is, we can understand why, if organs are used, they should be given rather than taken.

The Parts and the Whole

Human beings are animals, but not just animals. They are almost godlike in some of their powers, but are not gods. To honor and uphold the dignity of our humanity requires that we respect the peculiar nature of this in-between condition. A person is present to us and among us only as one who is embodied—even if also somehow more than body. And we, in turn, know ourselves not simply as a collection of organs but as a unified living being: not reason or will alone, not physical strength or spirit alone, but an integrated union of body, mind, will, and spirit.

If we first see how troubling even the giving is, we can understand why, if organs are used, they should be given rather than taken.

Thus, as neurologist-psychologist Erwin Straus once wrote, the truth that "only with eyes can we see" does not mean that we see with the eyes. On the contrary, it is the person, that unified living being, who sees. "Seeing is," as Straus put it, "located neither in the eye nor in the retina, nor in the optic nerve . . . the brain does not see." It is the person who sees. For certain limited purposes, we may think of or reduce the embodied person to a collection of parts, thinking of the person (from below, as it were) simply as the sum total of those parts. But we do not know either ourselves or others that way.

All organ transplantation, therefore, even when organs are given, not taken or purchased, invites us to think of ourselves and others in ways that risk the loss of the full meaning of our embodied humanity. All organ transplantation—even when undertaken for the best of reasons and even when justified—remains troubling. It tempts us to think of the body, in terms Paul Ramsey used, as just an "ensemble of parts," just a resource.

The Gift and the Giver

But a gift cannot so easily be severed from its giver. When an organ is freely given, that gift—like all gifts—carries with it the presence of the giver and directs our attention back to one who is not just a collection of alienable parts, but a unified living being. Indeed, what the donor gives is not simply an organ, but himself or herself. The gift can never be entirely severed or alienated from the giver. (Which is why, for example, we would think it wrong for a living donor to give an unpaired vital organ, such as the heart. The gift would undermine the very integrity of bodily life that it aimed to express.)

What the donor gives is not simply an organ, but himself or herself.

Taking organs, however, even under the somewhat euphemistic rubric of presumed consent, is a quite different matter. Although it does not alienate the organ from the person as decisively as would a system of buying and selling organs, it does go a long way toward treating persons as handy repositories of interchangeable parts. Learning to think of ourselves and others that way would be the true human tragedy and may still, just barely, be "an avoidable human tragedy"—to adapt Prime Minister Brown's words to my own quite different purpose.

We will avoid it, though, only to the degree that we cease to be simply cheerleaders in the cause of transplantation and regain, instead, an older wisdom of and about the meaning of the body. Fortified in that way, and aware of what is troubling about all organ transplantation, we will be better able to think about how it may be done rightly and how it should not be done even in the name of avoiding tragedy.

CHAPTER 3

Are Reproductive Technologies Ethical?

Overview: Reproductive Ethics

Marcia Clemmitt

Marcia Clemmitt is a journalist who covers economic, social, and health care issues in Washington, D.C. She is editor in chief of Medicine & Health, *a health policy publication.*

After 33-year-old Nadya Suleman, a mother of six, gave birth to octuplets on Jan. 26 [2009], the California fertility specialist who treated her was summoned to appear before the Medical Board of California. The board—which can revoke physicians' licenses for egregious misconduct—is investigating whether Michael Kamrava, head of the West Coast IVF Clinic in Beverly Hills, violated accepted standards of medical practice when he implanted at least six embryos in Suleman during in vitro fertilization (IVF) treatment in 2008, leading to the multiple birth. [Kamrava was accused of gross negligence in 2010, with a decision about his medical license still pending.]

Multiple Births

Suleman has told reporters that all 14 of her children were conceived using IVF—a high-tech treatment in which eggs are fertilized in the laboratory, then implanted into a woman's uterus for gestation—and that six embryos were implanted in each of her six pregnancies, although she's had only two multiple births: the octuplets and a set of twins. But professional guidelines from the American Society for Reproductive Medicine recommend implanting only one or two embryos in younger women, such as Suleman, because of the high risk multiple births pose to children and mothers.

Multiple-birth babies, including twins, have a significantly higher risk for developing severe, debilitating disabilities such as chronic lung diseases or cerebral palsy, which occurs six times more often among twins and 20 times more often in triplets than it does in single babies.

The cost to the health care system of multiple births is enormous. "The cost of caring for the octuplets would probably cover more than a year of providing IVF for everyone in L.A. County who needed it," says David L. Keefe, professor of obstetrics and gynecology at the University of South Florida, in Tampa. "The likelihood that some of those kids will get cerebral palsy means they'll need a lifetime of care."

Insurance Coverage for Reproductive Technologies

The high-profile Suleman case has spurred calls for government regulation of fertility medicine—sometimes called assisted reproductive technologies, or ART. Like U.S. medicine generally, ART is not regulated by the federal government and only lightly supervised by state agencies. Since 1978—when the world's first IVF baby, Louise Brown, was born in England—more than 3 million ART babies have been born worldwide, and some experts and ethicists fear the field's rapid expansion leaves too much room for abuses.

Others argue that lack of insurance coverage for IVF is the biggest problem with ART in the United States. Fertility treatments can cost more than $12,000 per cycle, pushing cash-strapped would-be parents to opt for the higher-risk, multiple-embryo implantation to increase their chances of a pregnancy.

The cost to the health care system of multiple births is enormous.

By contrast, in most European countries—where IVF procedures are paid for through universal health care systems—doctors generally implant only one fertilized embryo at a time. In Sweden and Finland, for instance, where the procedure is covered by insurance, doctors perform single-embryo implantations 70 percent and 60 percent of the time, respectively, compared to only 3.3 percent of the time in the United States.

In fact, some European governments prohibit multiple-embryo transfers for women under 36 and limit older women to no more than two embryos per cycle. As a result, "Triplets have virtually disappeared in Europe," a Danish doctor told European colleagues at a 2006 fertility conference.

The Issue of Regulation

Self-regulation of ART in the United States clearly isn't working, said Marcy Darnovsky, associate executive director of the Oakland, Calif.-based Center for Genetics and Society, which advocates for responsible use of genetic technologies. According to the federal Centers for Disease Control and Prevention (CDC), to which ART clinics must report data, 80 percent of programs do not strictly follow American Society for Reproductive Medicine guidelines, making government regulation "long overdue," she said.

"In reproductive matters, individuals are making decisions [that affect] not just themselves, but . . . others as well," which makes regulation appropriate, said Johns Hopkins University scholars Franco Furger and Francis Fukuyama. Reproductive medicine is headed toward giving prospective parents "a range of . . . techniques to make specific choices about a baby's health and sex and eventually about other attributes," said Furger, a research professor, and Fukuyama, a professor of international political economy, both at the Paul H. Nitze School of Advanced International Studies in Washington, D.C. "It would be misguided to take a wait-and-see attitude."

Industrialized countries that pay for IVF through their universal health care systems strictly regulate which services may be provided, says Susannah Baruch, director for law and policy at the Genetics and Public Policy Center, a think tank at John Hopkins funded by the Pew Charitable Trusts. The services typically include preimplantation genetic diagnosis (PGD)—genetic testing of embryos. While PGD to detect serious genetic illnesses is conducted routinely, many countries strictly limit other PGD uses, such as selecting a child's gender, because they aren't considered in the public interest, she says.

However, in the United States—even though U.S. reproductive-medicine experts roundly criticize Kamrava's implantation of multiple embryos in the Suleman case—many ART experts also argue that government regulation of the industry is not necessarily a solution.

Outlier Cases and Law

Suleman's case is much more of an outlier today than it would have been 15 years ago, when it wasn't unusual to have six embryos transferred, says Josephine Johnston, a research scholar at the Hastings Center for bioethics research in Garrison, N.Y. "I would have bet money that it was not IVF" that led to the octuplet birth, she says, but the use of ovary-stimulating drugs—a much cheaper, far less controllable method of assisted reproductive technology.

Opposition to regulation might drop considerably if insurance covered IVF and other artificial reproductive procedures.

Multiple-embryo implantation is being phased out as ART technologies improve, Johnston says, and six-embryo implantation is "so far outside the guidelines it's amazing that a physician would do it."

Such hair-raising cases are virtually always outliers and shouldn't be used to hastily enact laws, some analysts say.

For example, ever since artificial insemination was introduced, sperm banks have promised would-be parents a genetic lineage of intelligence, athleticism and good looks for babies born from donor sperm, says R. Alta Charo, a professor of law and bioethics at the University of Wisconsin Law School. But "it hasn't undermined Western culture as we know it," she says. "So why do we think that people are very likely to go through much more onerous PGD to choose traits?" Very few will try to use it to enhance their baby's intelligence or appearance, so there would be little point in prohibiting such behavior, she says.

A recent study by New York University's Langone Medical Center supports Charo's view somewhat. Of 999 patients who completed a survey on traits they thought warranted use of PGD screening, solid majorities named potential conditions such as mental retardation, blindness, deafness, heart disease and cancer. Only 10 percent said they might use PGD to choose a child with exceptional athletic ability and 12.6 percent [said] high intelligence.

"People are after different things" in calling for ART regulation, making legislation difficult, Charo says. Some may want limits on the number of embryos implanted per cycle, but most are calling for rules to enforce "personal morality," such as whether gay couples should become parents or whether lower-income mothers should be allowed to have very large families, Charo says. "We must then ask why we would regulate these [reproductive] personal choices differently from other personal choices."

ART-related law would likely be based on the unusual cases that make headlines, "and bad cases make bad policy," she says.

The High Cost of Reproductive Technologies

Opposition to regulation might drop considerably if insurance covered IVF and other artificial reproduction procedures, but today only 12 states require such coverage.

For instance, limitations on multiple-embryo implantations might be acceptable if insurance covered several single-
embryo implantations for all patients who have experienced
six months of proven infertility, suggests Ronald M. Green, a
professor of ethics and human values at Dartmouth College.

Because of the high cost of IVF treatments, the lack of insurance coverage has deprived "the vast majority of the middle
class" in America, as well as the poor, from the modern ART
"revolution," says Keefe at the University of South Florida.
"Once you have the middle class covered, then I have no
trouble saying, 'We're not going to pay'" for multiple-embryo
implantation.

Furthermore, the procedure doesn't have to cost $12,000
per cycle, as evidenced by the lower amounts accepted by IVF
clinics when insurance companies that are required to cover
the procedure negotiate lower fees, he says. "It's a lot cheaper
[for society] to pay for IVF at $3,000 or $4,000 per procedure
and deliver only singletons," thus avoiding the harrowing
medical problems and high costs associated with multiple
births, he says.

Mandating coverage not only reduces the number of multiple births but also increases access for the middle class. "I
practiced in Massachusetts and Rhode Island [which require
coverage], where sheet metal workers and heiresses from New-
port" mingled at IVF clinics because insurance picked up the
tab, Keefe says.

However, not all fertility doctors would opt into a fully insured system, says Dawn Gannon, director of professional
outreach for RESOLVE, the National Infertility Association,
which advocates that insurance companies treat infertility like
any other medical condition. For example, when New Jersey
mandated coverage, in 2001, "some clinics didn't take insurance at all, and some started taking it and then stopped," she
says, because "they got less money per procedure."

Issues About Insurance Coverage

If the United States enacts universal health care coverage, advocates for the infertile hope ART will be covered as it is in other industrialized countries.

But universal coverage would still leave thorny issues unsettled, such as whether taxpayer subsidies should support ART for unmarried women or women over 40. For older women, the debate centers on whether it is appropriate for health insurance to subsidize an infertility problem that is the result of natural aging and not the result of a medical condition. Also, pregnancy is riskier for both the older mother and the child.

Outlier cases like that of the California octuplets quickly spur vociferous calls for government limits on in vitro fertilization.

Earlier in IVF's history, many clinicians routinely refused ART to single women, older women, lesbians and, in some cases, poor people. A 1993 survey of Finnish ART clinics found that many doctors "preferred not to treat either lesbian or single women," arguing that they "wanted to protect children from having inappropriate parents, primarily 'bad mothers,'" according to Maili Malin, a medical sociologist at Finland's National Public Health Institute. A single woman's marital status and "wish to have a child" were both "considered indications of . . . questionable mental health."

Whatever the outcome, the coverage debate will generate intense emotion. "So much of your life feels out of control when you want a child but find that you can't have one," says Jan Elman Stout, a clinical psychologist in Chicago. "This is often the very first challenge that people encounter in their lives that, no matter how hard they work at it, it may not work out for them."

Issues in Fertility Medicine

As ethicists, lawmakers and physicians debate how best to provide access and oversight for reproductive medicine, here are some of the questions being asked:

Should fertility medicine be regulated more vigorously?

Should a mother of six with limited income be allowed to give birth to eight additional children through IVF? If a man donates sperm that results in hundreds of babies—technically making them all half brothers and sisters—should the offspring be given the identity of their biological father so they won't end up dating or marrying a half-sibling? Is a father whose child was the product of donated egg and sperm liable for child support if the couple divorces?

These are just a handful of the sticky ethical questions that have emerged from the brave, new world of sperm and egg donation.

Of course, outlier cases like that of the California octuplets quickly spur vociferous calls for government limits on in vitro fertilization. And others say the well-being of patients demands at least some rules. Finally, since many ART-related questions wind up in court, judges say they need more legislative guidance than the current case-by-case approach being used to settle IVF cases.

"No matter what one thinks of artificial insemination, and—as now appears in the not-too-distant future, cloning and even gene splicing—courts are still going to be faced with the problem of determining legal parentage," declared a unanimous California Court of Appeals ruling in the 1998 case *Buzzanca v. Buzzanca.* "Courts can continue to make decisions on an ad hoc basis . . . or the legislature can act to improve a broader order which . . . would bring some predictability to those who seek to make use of artificial reproductive techniques," said the justices in a case involving a divorcing husband who claimed no financial responsibility for his daughter, conceived from donor egg and sperm and borne by a surrogate mother.

Support for Government Regulation

Creating a federal-government registry of information on egg and sperm donors would give adults born from donated gametes (sperms or eggs) access to their genetic history in order to prevent half-siblings from marrying each other. It would also allow limits on the numbers of children created through one person's donations, said Naomi Cahn, a research professor at the George Washington University Law School. In England, no more than 10 children can be created from a single donor's sperm.

The federal government should exercise more aggressively the authority it already has to oversee the safety and efficacy of some ART technologies, say some experts.

For instance, inserting one woman's egg into another woman's body is arguably a type of tissue transplant—a procedure over which the Food and Drug Administration (FDA) has jurisdiction but has been lax in regulating, says the University of Wisconsin's Charo. "That's an appropriate place to step in to ask whether we have assurance of safety for the stuff that's being developed," she says.

The FDA has a role in determining whether genetic tests are safe and whether they work or are medically useful, says Baruch of the Genetics and Public Policy Center. For instance, many labs manufacture genetic tests that they don't market to other companies—called "homebrew" tests—but the FDA "has chosen not to regulate them," she says. "We believe that they have the authority" and would like to see them do it.

Genetic testing of embryos—preimplantation genetic diagnosis or PGD, which requires permanent removal of one cell from an eight-cell embryo—is much more technically difficult than other forms of genetic testing, but gets less government scrutiny, according to Baruch's organization. And, the center points out, even the general quality standards for laboratories under the federal Clinical Laboratory Improvement Amendments of 1988 are not being applied to PGD labs.

But aside from testing the safety and efficacy of medical products and drugs, the U.S. government does not, in general, regulate the practice of medicine, says Wisconsin's Charo. "That being the case, the issue of regulating fertility clinics actually becomes, 'Should they be regulated differently from the rest of medicine?'" she says. "It would be difficult to make that case."

Criticism of Government Regulation

"Muddling through" without regulation "is a respectable policy option, especially for a pragmatic people faced with irreconcilable moral quandaries" such as those often posed by ART, said John A. Robertson, a professor at the University of Texas School of Law in Austin. "This non-system 'system' has served well to date—even if not all the time and never perfectly—both in other contexts and for assisted reproduction." The current system can deal with even thorny issues, he adds, such as questions surrounding the "genetic screening of embryos . . . and the other edge technologies looming ahead."

Furthermore, he pointed out, the President's Council on Bioethics appointed by George W. Bush examined the ART field for more than a year and found that the biggest problems were "on the margins, not at the core." The panel recommended only "tinker[ing] with ways to get more data" and making professional self-regulation more effective.

National Infertility Association [RESOLVE] Executive Director Barbara L. Collura also advocates caution in regulating ART. While limiting the number of embryos implanted per cycle may seem like a no-brainer, she says, such a rule could be prohibitively difficult because of the wide variety of medical conditions that could occur. For example, she argues, while the American Society for Reproductive Medicine strongly recommends transferring only one—or at most two—embryos at a time, if a woman has already had three or four cycles of IVF and her embryo quality is poor, a doctor could easily justify implanting multiple embryos. "How do you put that into a law?" she asks.

And some fertility doctors argue that they're already more regulated than most other U.S. physicians. "FDA put in tons of rules a few years ago . . . [that] added hundreds of dollars to the cost," says John Jain, who heads a fertility clinic in Santa Monica, Calif. The guidelines, which mainly dealt with disease-testing of donated gametes, involved "viruses I've never seen in my life." He fears that other regulations "will add to the already exorbitant cost."

David L. Rosenfeld, director of the Center for Human Reproduction at the North Shore-Long Island Jewish Health System in Manhasset, N.Y., makes the same point. "We're already highly scrutinized," he says. Thanks to the CDC's fertility-clinic database, he adds, reproductive-medicine specialists are "the only physicians in the country whose numbers are published nationally."

Some fertility doctors argue that they're already more regulated than most other U.S. physicians.

Sanctions for outlier physicians already exist at state licensing boards such as the one scrutinizing Suleman's doctor, says Jain. "As a physician, how far do I need to be policed? If there are poor outcomes, a level of public scrutiny" emerges—as it has in the octuplets' case—which helps rein in doctors inclined to go too far, he says.

Finally, some doctors contend that having light government oversight allows U.S. medicine to advance rapidly.

"We are probably leaders in the field of reproductive medicine because we can advance without government interference," says Angeline Beltsos, medical director of the Chicago-based Fertility Centers of Illinois. "Creating guidelines is critical, but legislating is dangerous." ...

The Issue of Doctor Refusal to Treat

Should doctors be able to refuse ART services to gay, older or single people?

The University of South Florida's Keefe says that a gay, male couple came into his clinic in Tampa and were at their wits' end. They had been to several assisted reproductive technology (ART) clinics seeking services, only to be turned away because center officials said they didn't want to be known as a clinic that welcomed gay families.

"These were taxpaying Americans who were very loving to each other, and they'd been bounced from one place to another," says Keefe, who helped the couple conceive a child using donor eggs and a surrogate.

Indeed, some doctors refuse to provide IVF to would-be parents because of their single, gay or elder status, usually citing religious or ethical reasons—or, in the case of older parents—concern about the long-term welfare of the child.

Some ethicists say clinics must first consider the welfare of the children in choosing whom to treat, and questions of religion and conscience figure strongly in such decisions.

In a 2007 report, the ethics committee of the American College of Obstetricians and Gynecologists described a California physician who refused to perform artificial insemination for a lesbian couple, "prompted by religious beliefs and disapproval of lesbians having children." In reproductive medicine, the report said, "health care providers may find that providing indicated, even standard, care would present for them a personal moral problem—a conflict of conscience." The committee upheld doctors' rights to refuse care on those grounds, but said doctors who refuse service must refer patients to other providers.

Because the desire to raise children is not a medical need, physicians may ethically refuse to help people seeking IVF services, argued Julien S. Murphy, a professor of philosophy at the University of Southern Maine. In general, "it is assumed that physicians have a duty to treat 'medical conditions,'" she wrote, "but addressing the fulfillment of reproductive possibilities" opened up by new technology "is an optional matter."

Support for Doctor Refusal

A 2005 survey of fertility doctors found that only 44 percent believed doctors do not have the right to decide who is fit to procreate, according to *Everything Conceivable: How Assisted Reproduction Is Changing Our World* author [Liza] Mundy. Nearly half the physicians surveyed said they'd refuse services to a gay couple, 40 percent said they'd refuse service to a couple on welfare who wanted to pay with Social Security disability checks and 20 percent said they would turn away a single woman.

Some ethicists say clinics must first consider the welfare of the children in choosing whom to treat.

Such ethical debates are not limited to the United States. Arguing for a ban on ART for single or lesbian women, a member of the Danish parliament stated that such women have "completely, freely chosen to live" in a manner that "cannot naturally produce children," making providing ART to them "completely against nature, artificial and absurd."

Many English fertility clinics will not serve single women, said Clare Murray, a psychologist at City University London. "Clinics treat lesbian couples at the drop of a hat, but still won't treat single women. They're the pariahs of the assisted-reproduction field."

And University of Pennsylvania bioethicist Arthur Caplan argues that physicians have every right—and perhaps a moral duty—to refuse ART for people who are too old. He was commenting on the 2005 Caesarian-section [C-section] birth of a daughter to 66-year-old Adriana Iliescu, an unmarried professor in Bucharest, Romania.

Such pregnancies are medically risky, Caplan noted. For instance, in Iliescu's IVF treatments, she initially had a miscarriage, then a stillbirth and, finally, a live child born prematurely from a "life-threatening emergency C-section." Furthermore, he pointed out, when the daughter enters high school, Iliescu will be 80, too old to raise a teenager to adulthood.

Caplan said he would refuse ART to single people over 65 or to a couple with one member who is 65 or older, making their total age higher than 130, and to any woman age 55 or older who could not pass "a rigorous physical examination."

Criticism of Doctor Refusal

But other physicians say that—aside from screening out patients with severe mental disorders—deciding who may have children should not be up to the doctor. "How does that become my responsibility?" says Beltsos, of the Fertility Centers of Illinois. The case of octuplet-mother Suleman is "a tough one, but just because I might think it's inappropriate or irresponsible to have 14 kids, does that mean I can decide for someone else? Where does the line get drawn?"

Other physicians say that ... deciding who may have children should not be up to the doctor.

As for worrying about the welfare of the child, the Hastings Center's Johnston says that IVF clinics deal with people who fervently want children. "This is not the population where the real child welfare problem is," she says. "We take wanting a child as a kind of placeholder for doing a pretty good job with the child," so she says she probably wouldn't support clinics adding child welfare considerations to their protocols for accepting ART patients.

In August 2008, the California Supreme Court ruled that denying ART services to a lesbian constitutes unlawful discrimination under a law requiring businesses to guarantee all persons "full and equal accommodations."

In *North Coast Women's Care Medical Group, Inc. v. [San Diego County] Superior Court* the court ruled in favor of Guadalupe Benitez, a lesbian in a long-term relationship who sued the facility after two physicians refused to artificially inseminate her and referred her to another clinic. The doctors argued that their rights to religious liberty would be violated if they were required to provide ART to all comers. But the court said the state's civil rights law trumps the religious-liberty claim and requires the clinic to either offer ART to no one or have at least one physician on staff who will provide it to all clients.

An American Society for Reproductive Medicine ethics committee declared in 2006 that, "as a matter of ethics, we believe the ethical duty to treat persons with equal respect requires that fertility programs treat single persons and gay and lesbian couples equally with married couples in determining which services to provide."

Unmarried Individuals and Homosexuals Should Have Access to Reproductive Technologies

The Ethics Committee of the American Society for Reproductive Medicine

The Ethics Committee of the American Society for Reproductive Medicine makes ethics recommendations on behalf of the non-profit organization, which offers multidisciplinary information, education, advocacy, and standards in the field of reproductive medicine.

A family traditionally consisted of a man, married to a woman, and their children. The father was the provider, and the mother stayed at home to raise coitally [through sexual intercourse] conceived children. This idealized concept never was fully realized and has changed markedly in recent years as a result of high divorce and out-of-wedlock birth rates, adoption, assisted reproduction, recognition of women's rights, the gay rights movement, the legalization of same-sex marriage in some jurisdictions, and other social and economic factors.

The Changing Nature of Reproduction

Although the majority of births still occur within the context of heterosexual married couples, variations abound. Marital reproduction no longer is solely coital and may include a third-party gamete [sperm or egg] donor or a surrogate carrier. The incidence of births to single or unmarried persons also has grown, including among never-married, college-educated, professional women. A growing number of professional women without male partners have chosen to have children, sometimes with the help of donor insemination. In 2007, nearly 40% of all U.S. births were to unmarried women.

In addition to the shift toward assisted reproduction and the growing frequency of out-of-wedlock births, societal acceptance of gays and lesbians also has changed. The U.S. Supreme Court has ruled that criminal bans on homosexual activity are unconstitutional. With the exception of military service and marriage in most jurisdictions, discrimination on the basis of sexual orientation no longer appears to be a permissible basis for governmental discrimination. In addition, approximately 15 U.S. states (including California, Illinois, Massachusetts, New Jersey, New York, Minnesota, and Wisconsin) now ban private discrimination on the basis of sexual orientation in public accommodations and services.

Accompanying these changes has been an increase in the number of unmarried persons, including those who are gay or lesbian, who seek medical assistance to reproduce. Although gays and lesbians often have had children when married to persons of the opposite sex, a notable trend is for lesbian women and couples and, increasingly, for single and coupled gay men, to have offspring, most commonly through some form of assisted reproduction. Currently in the United States, there are an estimated 6 to 14 million children being raised by at least one gay or lesbian parent, usually as a result of a heterosexual relationship.

Although the majority of births still occur within the context of heterosexual married couples, variations abound.

The ethical debate over whether a program may—or must—assist single women and men as well as gay and lesbian couples to have children depends on the balance among three important values. The first is the reproductive interest of unmarried and gay and lesbian persons. The second is the protection of the welfare of offspring. The third is whether professional autonomy, combined with prevailing law, provides a limit on the duty not to discriminate on the basis of marital status or sexual orientation.

The Reproductive Interests of Unmarried Persons and Gays and Lesbians

Although reproduction traditionally has been regarded as an aspect of marriage, single persons and gays and lesbians also have interests in having and rearing offspring even if they are not married or attracted to persons of the opposite sex. Some women and men have no permanent partner, yet are interested in having and rearing children as single parents. Many gays and lesbians already have had children with persons of the opposite sex and share rearing or have sole custody when those relationships end. If they have not adopted or had children, they may wish as single or coupled persons to have offspring for the same reasons of intimacy, companionship, nurturance, family, and legacy that motivate reproduction generally.

Given the importance to individuals of having children, there is no sound basis for denying to single persons and gays and lesbians the same rights to reproduce that other individuals enjoy. No state penalizes reproduction per se by unmarried persons, whether achieved coitally or with medical assistance. All states allow unmarried persons, including gays and lesbians, to be foster parents, and all states but four allow single persons and gay and lesbian couples to adopt. Legal developments make it unlikely that the government could constitutionally ban assisted reproduction to single persons or to gay and lesbian couples, even if same-sex marriage or civil unions are not recognized legally. Moral condemnation of homosexuality or single parenthood is not itself an acceptable basis for limiting child rearing or reproduction.

The Issue of Protecting Offspring

Many persons who oppose reproduction by single persons or gay or lesbian couples do so out of concern for the welfare of intended offspring. They argue that the best rearing environment for a child is a two-person, married, heterosexual family and are reluctant to assist or facilitate any different arrangement. They may find that some nonmarital arrangements are compatible with a child's welfare, whereas others are not. For example, some fertility programs may treat lesbian, but not gay male couples, or single women, but not single men.

Moral condemnation of homosexuality or single parenthood is not itself an acceptable basis for limiting child rearing or reproduction.

A closer look at the reasoning of opponents of assisted reproduction for unmarried persons or for gays and lesbians reveals that there are important differences in the positions taken. Those clinicians who will not treat single females, for example, may believe that fertility treatment should be restricted to married couples, that treatment should be for the infertile only, or that children need a father and a "normal upbringing." Others may believe that children of gay and lesbian mothers will experience social isolation and gender-identity or sexual-orientation problems. One concern with assisting single men to reproduce is that men are perceived as less caring or nurturing than women and that children need a "normal upbringing" with a mother. Some persons also have claimed that children of single men or of gay male couples are at greater risk for sexual abuse, pedophilia, or other mistreatment.

The evidence to date, however, cannot reasonably be interpreted to support such fears. A task force of the American Psychological Association has reviewed the existing data and found that fears that there would be a higher rate of psychological or social problems among children born in those settings could not be substantiated:

> Results of social science research have failed to confirm any of these concerns about children of lesbian and gay parents. . . . Research suggests that sexual identities (including gender identity, gender-role behavior, and sexual orientation) develop in much the same ways among children of lesbian mothers as they do among children of heterosexual parents. . . . Studies of other aspects of personal development (including personality, self-concept, and conduct) similarly reveal few differences between children of lesbian mothers and children of heterosexual parents. . . . Evidence also suggests that children of lesbian and gay parents have normal social relationships with peers and adults. . . . Overall results of research suggest that the development, adjustment, and well-being of children with lesbian and gay parents do not differ markedly from that of children with heterosexual parents.

With regard to outcomes for children of gay male couples, the task force found that fewer data were available. The literature that does exist, however, found no evidence that being raised by a gay father had any negative effect on children. Indeed, identified differences tended to favor the gay fathers. They were found to be more alert to children's needs and more nurturing in providing care than heterosexual fathers, who may see themselves primarily as the person providing financial security.

In sum, on the basis of the available evidence, we do not believe that one can reasonably claim that unmarried persons or gays and lesbians harm their children by reproducing outside of heterosexual marital relations. Children born in such situations do not appear to have appreciably worse lives than do children born to heterosexual married parents. Given the importance of reproduction to unmarried and gay and lesbian persons and the absence of harm to children from being reared by such parents, we find that programs act ethically in assisting unmarried persons or gays and lesbians to reproduce when they meet the same medical criteria for treatment as married heterosexuals.

Professional Autonomy and the Obligation to Treat Equally

Despite these social trends and these data, some persons still may view homosexuality as immoral or may oppose facilitating gay and lesbian or unmarried reproduction. As a result, fertility programs may differ in their willingness to provide reproductive services, regardless of the marital status or sexual orientation of prospective patients. Sometimes, the unwillingness to treat is based on religious or personal moral views about the propriety or desirability of unmarried persons or gays and lesbians having children. At other times it may reflect the administrative complications of working with egg donors or surrogate mothers that assistance to gay male individuals or couples entails.

We believe that the ethical duty to treat persons with equal respect requires that fertility programs treat single persons and gay and lesbian couples equally to heterosexual married couples.

As a matter of law, fertility programs may be prohibited from denying ART [assisted reproductive technology] services to patients on the basis of their marital status or sexual orientation. In 2008, the California Supreme Court ruled that refusal to treat a lesbian patient based on the physician's religious views violated state law. The court found that assertions of religious freedom are preempted by state law that prohibits discrimination in public accommodations based on sexual orientation. Since medical offices are considered public accommodations under civil rights laws, and about half of all states ban discrimination on the basis of marital status, with another third banning discrimination on the basis of sexual orientation, provider autonomy may not protect physicians who refuse ART services based on patient demographic characteristics.

As a matter of ethics, we believe that the ethical duty to treat persons with equal respect requires that fertility programs treat single persons and gay and lesbian couples equally to heterosexual married couples in determining which services to provide. Other professional organizations have expressed support for nondiscriminatory access to assisted reproduction, including the American College of Obstetricians and Gynecologists, which said of physicians who refuse to provide infertility services to same-sex couples:

> [A]llowing physicians to discriminate on the basis of sexual orientation would constitute a deeper insult, namely reinforcing the scientifically unfounded idea that fitness to parent is based on sexual orientation, and, thus, reinforcing the oppressed status of same-sex couples.

Unless other aspects of the situation also would disqualify heterosexual married couples or individuals from services, such as serious doubts about whether they will be fit or responsible child rearers, or the fact that the program does not offer anyone a desired service, for example, gestational surrogacy, we find no sound ethical basis for licensed professionals to deny reproductive services to unmarried or gay and lesbian persons.

Surrogacy Can Be an Ethical Solution to Infertility

Sudesh Kumar

Sudesh Kumar is an economic and regulatory affairs consultant based in London.

In this day and age where capitalism rules the world, there has been much debate over the commoditization of numerous once-sacred activities such as child birth. For a fixed price tag, you can now implant your spouse's and your gametes [eggs or sperm] into a third-party's womb and receive your child nine months later. However, opponents of surrogacy view the advent of surrogacy as the beginning of a slippery slope. By allowing couples to pay for the birth of healthy babies from the womb of a surrogate, some have felt that it is similar to selling the baby in the end, as money is transacted and what the couple receives is the baby. Others have argued that surrogate mothers undergo mental trauma as they are expected to give up the babies that have lived in their wombs for the past nine months because of a bond formed between them. This moral dilemma has also highlighted the legal problems surrounding surrogacy, especially if the surrogate mother decides to lay claims on the baby after its birth. There is debate too on the claim that surrogacy exploits the poor as only those in need of money would so willingly give up their wombs for others, subjecting themselves to the risk of maternal deaths that may be a problem in countries with poor or inadequate health care facilities. More extreme feminists even argued that surrogacy is similar to prostitution as women in both instances are sexually exploited for money.

Myths About Surrogacy

I would like to debunk some of these myths as I feel that there is a need and a place for surrogacy to exist in society. Firstly, it is important to note that as couples are becoming more educated, some put off procreation and settling down to start a family because they want to pursue their dreams or that high-flying career, thus they tend to experience fertility problems which become increasingly common with age. This creates a gaping difference between wants and ability. The couple who is financially stable has decided to start a family, but they are unable to because of biological reasons. This is where surrogacy fills the gap by enabling couples who have given up their childbearing years for financial security a real chance at having a family of their own. Although some may argue that there is always adoption to meet such a gap, it is undeniable that there is a preference for raising one's own flesh and blood instead of someone else's.

Secondly, surrogacy should not be seen as the commoditization of infants even though the end product of the whole surrogate pregnancy is the baby. In economics, a commodity is a unit that can substitute for another at all points, so each unit has no special intrinsic value. Thus, one cannot argue that the baby has become a commodity in surrogacy, as the baby is unique. In fact, the babies would not even exist, if not for the surrogacy. Surrogacy should be instead viewed as the payments to the individual for the gestational services provided to bring the client's bloodline into this world. Surrogate mothers are respected for such services, as surrogacy is a tedious and dangerous job which puts their lives on the line, so they should be fairly compensated. This brings us to the point on the mental trauma experienced by surrogate mothers after birth. Rather than to accept the common misperception that surrogates feel traumatized after relinquishment of their rights over the child, it has been challenged that an increasing majority feel empowered by their surrogacy experience.

Thirdly, clients would definitely choose healthy surrogates to bear their children, so the claim that surrogacy exploits the poor usually does not hold as clients are likely to decline a surrogate in abject poverty due to the unstable environment she is living in. Feminists who make the comparison to prostitution are preposterous as the underlying aim of both activities are different and should never be seen as a single entity together.

Surrogacy should not be seen as the commoditization of infants.

Avoiding Problems with Surrogacy

However, we do admit that there are thorny issues that have to be resolved here before we can fully embrace surrogacy. Although medical health care is becoming increasingly commonplace and advanced, there is always the risk that surrogates undertake to bring life into this world. In the event that something unfortunate does occur, will insurance policies cover the costs incurred or will they choose to argue that they are allowed to forgo the compensation as the surrogates chose to bear the children themselves, and hence created the opportunities for such mishaps to occur, where the risk was not initially calculated into the previous insurance premiums they were paying? There is also a problem of ownership over the baby that may arise due to the complexity and possibilities that may occur during the entire process. These include concerns like what happens if the surrogate fails to relinquish her rights over the child after the birth. In this respect, I feel that the surrogacy contract laws should be reviewed to enforce a mandate that the contracts may not require the woman who carries the baby to surrender it regardless, but in choosing to do so, she has to compensate the parents fairly. This should only be undertaken as a last resort as frequent occurrences of such would only serve to discredit surrogate mothers in general. Hence, rigorous counselling should be provided to both client and surrogate before legalising the transaction.

Rigorous counselling should be provided to both client and surrogate before legalising the transaction.

More complex situations may arise in a situation where the clients pass away during the course of the pregnancy. Should a surrogate be allowed to abort the fetus then as it is technically not hers and it would have perished together with the mother should the pregnancy have been borne by her? Yet, this is clearly not an option as such actions would be inhuman as it literally devalues and insults the sacredness of life. The infant may also be orphaned if the couple divorces each other and decides that neither is interested in taking care of the baby they once planned to have together; for example, the recent [2008] case where a baby girl was abandoned in India. She is the first surrogacy orphan after her parents divorced weeks before she was born and her mother refused to take her. The custody of the child born to an Indian surrogate mother and intended for a Japanese couple hangs in limbo after the pair divorced. Also, should the couple be allowed to terminate the pregnancy if the surrogate accidentally violates the terms and conditions of the surrogacy contract, resulting in unintended consequences on the well-being of the child? For example, is the couple paying for the surrogacy allowed to request for an abortion should the surrogate mother contract a disease like AIDS where there is an extremely high chance that it is directly passed to the infant? While this is an unfortunate situation, there is a huge conflict between all involved parties as everyone is impacted by the final decision undertaken. Thus, it is favourable to consider how to keep ourselves out of such problems first, before embracing surrogacy.

The infinite number of possibilities only compound the ethical and moral dilemmas encountered during the implementation of surrogacy as a primary means of enabling couples who wish to have children but are unable to do so. Even though to some the ends may not justify the means, we should look towards greater compromise in society and the creation of social safety nets to minimise such tragedies from happening in our search for other ways to taste the joy of having a family.

Fertility Doctors Are in No Position to Consider Children's Well-Being

Josephine Johnston

Josephine Johnston is a research scholar at the Hastings Center, an independent, nonpartisan, and nonprofit bioethics research institute.

Just over a week after her eight babies were delivered by caesarean section in a California hospital, Nadya Suleman explained to an NBC reporter that her extraordinary pregnancy was the result of in vitro fertilization [IVF]. Having conceived her first six children—four singletons and one set of twins—using IVF, Suleman said she visited her fertility doctor in 2008 and insisted that he transfer all of her six remaining frozen embryos at once. After warning her of the risks associated with a multiple birth, he'd done as she asked. All six embryos implanted, and two divided to create twins.

Reproductive Technologies and Multiple Births

Awe at the successful delivery of her children quickly turned to ire when the press discovered that Suleman not only has six children already, but is an unemployed single mother on public assistance. Many feel she has irresponsibly created more mouths than she can possibly feed, and that the taxpayers of California are going to be left holding the babies, as it were.

Like many familiar with the ins and outs of fertility treatment, I initially assumed that the octuplets resulted from Suleman's body "overreacting" to fertility medications. I guessed that her physician had either failed to monitor her

Josephine Johnston, "Judging Octomom," *Hastings Center Report*, vol. 39, no. 3, May/June 2009, pp. 23–25. Copyright © 2009 Hastings Center. Reproduced by permission.

egg development adequately before inseminating her, or that she had intercourse around the time her body released a large number of eggs. The idea that IVF—the most controllable form of assisted reproductive technology—had been used in such clear contravention of current professional guidelines and practice was almost unthinkable.

In the early years of IVF, it was not unusual to transfer six embryos to a woman in the hope that just one would successfully implant. But as the technology has improved, multiple births have become more frequent. While high-order multiples were welcomed by some patients, a few sued their physicians for the costs and harms to mothers and infants associated with complicated premature births. In 1992, the Centers for Disease Control and Prevention [CDC] began collecting statistics from fertility clinics and reporting clinic-specific success rates that highlighted not just the number of pregnancies achieved and infants born, but also the number and degree of multiple births. Among other goals, the CDC's reports aim to improve the safety of assisted reproduction technologies for women and their babies by pinpointing clinics that generate high numbers of multiples. As noted on the program's Web site, "Multiple birth is associated with poor infant and maternal health outcomes, including pregnancy complications, preterm delivery, low birth weight, congenital malformations, and infant death."

The American Society for Reproductive Medicine [ASRM] also seeks to reduce the number of multiples born to its members' patients. To this end it recommends that when treating women of Nadya Suleman's age (under thirty-five years) who have a favorable prognosis, physicians consider transferring only one and no more than two blastocysts (embryos at five or six days of development). There is clearly some wiggle room here—for example, if Suleman's doctor was transferring embryos at day three of development (which are less likely to survive than embryos that have developed in the lab to the blastocyst stage), he might have argued for transferring two or three rather than one or two. But in a thirty-three-year-old woman who had successfully used IVF already, transferring six embryos is so far beyond the guidelines as to ignore them completely. And maybe Suleman's physician did simply ignore them: As John [A.] Robertson points out . . . the guidelines have few teeth.

Patient Dispositional Authority

When everyone else is reducing the number of embryo transfers, how might we understand the decision of Suleman's physician to transfer six? Maybe he is simply unskilled—his clinic does have very low success rates, even by the crudest measure, so perhaps, based on his past performance, he expected fewer embryos to implant (and he likely did not expect two of them to twin).

As the technology has improved, multiple births have become more frequent.

Or maybe he was listening not to ASRM guidelines or evolutions in clinical practice, but to his patient. Just exactly how much control fertility patients should have over the procedures they undergo is hotly debated, in bioethics and beyond. Patients have what is known as "dispositional authority" over their embryos—they can decide whether unused embryos should be frozen, whether either parent can use them in the event of death or divorce, and whether unused frozen embryos should eventually be discarded, donated to other would-be parents, or donated to research. Good clinics ask their patients to consider these issues even before embryos are made.

But dispositional authority does not require physicians to accede to any and all patient demands. Suleman's physician would have been well within his legal and moral rights if he refused a request that so flagrantly violated professional guidelines. Indeed, I believe he *should* have refused to transfer all six embryos at once because to do so was so very dangerous for both Suleman and her babies. The harder question, in my view, is whether he should have refused to treat her at all on account of her circumstances, even if she had come to him with a more reasonable request.

Fertility Clinics and Adoption Agencies

Many have noted that fertility clinics primarily treat the men and women having trouble conceiving, rather than the children they hope to bear. And many have contrasted the way fertility clinics frame their services and understand their goals with the way adoption agencies operate. Some in bioethics have argued that Suleman's fertility doctor should have turned her away on account of her existing obligations and her financial status; in essence, they contend that something like an adoption standard should have been applied to her.

Fertility clinics aim to help people have babies, while adoption services aim to place parentless children in safe, loving homes. In the fertility clinic, doctors perform detailed assessments of both patient fertility and physical readiness to gestate a baby. They may learn something about the intended parent or parents' psychological well-being, but clinics do not require parent training or a home study, nor do social workers assess would-be parents' fitness, run criminal background checks, speak with references, or inquire into financial stability. While one can argue that the cost of fertility procedures can act as a de facto financial screen—most patients are probably financially stable enough to have adequate insurance or to be able to pay out-of-pocket—it's a very light and potentially uninformative substitute for the kind of detailed information adoption agencies gather.

Because adoption cases usually concern an existing child, state and private agencies may be legally—and, I would argue, morally—bound to investigate would-be parents. But while ASRM's ethics committee advises that physicians may decide to withhold services if they believe patients will be unable to provide adequate child rearing, it also makes clear that physicians are not morally obliged to do so except "when significant harm to future children is likely." This seems a difficult standard to meet.

Fertility clinics are not suited to judge who will make a good parent.

Determining Parental Fitness

If the United States ever decided to regulate assisted reproduction, it could mandate that future children's welfare be taken into account, as is done in the United Kingdom. But as ASRM's ethics committee notes, clinics are not currently well equipped to make such assessments, and when they do, their judgments may betray discrimination: In the past, they have been held legally and morally blameworthy for denying services to single people and gay men and women.

Fertility patients in the United States are treated more or less like anyone else trying to conceive: No preapproval is required. And this is probably the way it should stay. Fertility clinics are not suited to judge who will make a good parent. ASRM is right that clinics should refuse to provide treatment to individuals or couples it learns have "uncontrolled psychiatric illness, substance abuse, on-going physical or emotional abuse, or a history of perpetuating physical or emotional abuse" (none of which seem to apply to Suleman). But unless we have good evidence that the fertility industry is creating a child welfare problem, I see no reason to require clinics to probe deeper into their patients' circumstances than they currently do. While I agree that assisted reproduction invites a more careful approach to procreation than is taken "in the wild," I would be very suspicious of a new rule concerning parental fitness that stems from one highly unusual case. We know there are children in need of safer, healthier, and more supportive homes in this country, but we have little reason to think that asking fertility clinics to assess the fitness of would-be parents would do anything to address that problem.

Unmarried Individuals and Homosexuals Do Not Have a Right to Reproductive Technologies

Jennifer Roback Morse

Jennifer Roback Morse is the founder and president of the Ruth Institute, a nonprofit educational institute promoting lifelong married love. She is also the senior research fellow in economics at the Acton Institute for the Study of Religion and Liberty and author of Smart Sex: Finding Life-Long Love in a Hook-up World.

In Vista, California, an infertility clinic with a policy of artificially inseminating only married women is being sued by a lesbian woman for sexual orientation discrimination. In Indiana, a law was introduced and quickly withdrawn that would have confined the use of artificial reproductive technologies to married couples.

The superficial appeal of the lesbian's case is that having a baby is a right, from which no one can be excluded, no matter what their marital status. The ill-fated Indiana law was shot down because its opponents appealed to the same intuitive sense, widely felt by Americans, that people have a right to have a baby.

The Right to Have a Child

There is some legal precedent for believing that procreation is a fundamental right. The Supreme Court has held (in *Skinner v. Oklahoma* [1942]) that sterilization cannot be used as a criminal penalty because the right to have children is a fundamental right, but this right surely cannot mean that anyone who wants a baby is entitled to a baby, and that someone is required to give them one.

Let me be blunt: There is no right to a child, because a child is not an object to which other people have rights. If that were true, then parents would be owners of their children, rather than their stewards or guardians. The well-being of the child could be, and would be, sacrificed to the "rights" of the parents. If we are born as objects to which other people have rights, when do we become persons with rights of our own, and why does the woman's "right" to have a child trump the child's right to have a father?

The family courts do not typically use the language of rights, even for children already born to specific and identifiable individuals. They usually do not say, "These parents have a right to this child." Even when they use the term "parental rights," these are not like property rights to cars and refrigerators. Children are not chattel. A person cannot dispose of his children, or write a contract to give up these rights. If anyone has a right to anything, it is the child.

We must distinguish between "the right to have a child" in the sense of possession and the "right to have a child" in the sense of procreation. There is one coherent way to imagine a right to procreate. Two people of the opposite sex can come together to conceive a child, without permission from the state or anyone else. People do it all the time.

There is no right to a child, because a child is not an object to which other people have rights.

To put it another way: Every individual is sterile. No one can have a baby by himself. Each human infant has two parents, one male and one female. Therefore, any right to have a child should be held by a couple, not by an individual who wishes to be a parent.

A Couple's Right

This right of procreation a married couple holds is, quite literally, a natural right. No one has to help the couple produce the child: They can do that all by themselves. In fact, one of the great problems every society has to solve is discouraging reproduction in certain circumstances, precisely because producing babies is all too easy and natural to do.

Every known society has developed some social institution for defining the appropriate types of reproductive couplings. Whatever the specific rules, formal and informal, all societies limit the appropriate context for both sexual activity and childbearing. As long as a couple meets a society's criteria, as the natural parents of the child, they obtain the rights to exercise the full complement of parental rights it grants.

This universal social institution is, of course, marriage. Nobody grants a married couple the right to make babies; it is inherent in their marriage.

It does not follow that the natural right of a married couple to have babies extends to random couplings of individuals. Nor does the entitlement of married couples to procreate naturally generate a right for anyone to be artificially inseminated. No one, married or otherwise, is entitled to the assistance of others in becoming a parent.

The Right of the Child

The virtue of recognizing the natural right of a married couple to procreate is that this arrangement best protects the rights of the most vulnerable, namely, the child. What is owed to the child? The child's most basic entitlement is the right to be born into a home with both a mother and a father who love him and each other. This gives the child at least the possibility of a relationship with both parents.

In the vast majority of cases, this basic right of relationship will involve provision for the child's material needs because the natural parents have the greatest incentive and opportunity to meet those needs. The right of relationship is widely viewed as more fundamental than the right to material support in this sense: Being poor is not ordinarily grounds for removing children from their natural parents. The state will not remove children unless the parents are grossly negligent or abusive.

No one, married or otherwise, is entitled to the assistance of others in becoming a parent.

Individuals may appear to have the same procreation rights as married couples. The belief that they do creates the widespread sympathy for the lesbian in the doctors' conscience case, and the antipathy against the proposed Indiana restriction on artificial reproductive technology. But there is no individual right to have a child, and the state should decline to "discover" or invent one.

Divided Parents

Unfortunately, forty years of public discussion, policy, and the courts' decisions about "reproductive rights" have been muddled by exactly the failure to take this basic biological fact into account. The language of rights has been used to divide the reproductive pair into individuals.

For instance, the feminist chant, "a woman's body, a woman's choice," not only forgets the interests of the child, it ignores the interests of the male partner in the reproductive enterprise. While a man's body does not give birth to a child, his body may legally be pressed into eighteen to twenty years of service to support the child. Public policies that support a low-income woman and her child if she is unmarried undermine the father's participation. These state policies replace the male half of the reproductive unit with a government check.

The Supreme Court disaggregated the married couple into an association of two individuals when it asserted an individual's right to obtain and use contraceptives in the 1972 *Eisenstadt v. Baird* case. "Whatever the rights of the individual to access to contraceptives may be, the rights must be the same for the married and unmarried alike," the Court declared, defining the married couple as "an association of two individuals each with a separate intellectual and emotional makeup."

Surely there is a compelling social good in attaching both biological parents to each other and to the child.

The Court concluded: "If the right of privacy means anything, it is the right to be free from unwarranted government intrusions into matters so fundamentally affecting a person as the decision whether to bear or beget a child."

Married Couples Only

But privacy is not the only issue at stake in childbearing. The integrity of the couple as a mated pair is also worth protecting. Giving legal recognition to the couple upholds the adults' interests in parenting their jointly conceived child, as well as the child's interest in having a relation with both parents.

Once we realize that the "right to have a baby" is not and cannot be an individual right, but inherently resides in a couple, we have to ask ourselves: what kind of couple? Surely there is a compelling social good in attaching both biological parents to each other and to the child. This satisfies the child's entitlement to a relationship with both parents and meets the social good that the child be provided for.

Just as surely, it makes no sense to assign the parental rights to couples who mate with each other more or less at random and who demonstrate no willingness or ability to create a common life that they could share with a child. This is why the Indiana law, limiting the use of sperm banks to married couples, was on the right track.

Unfortunately, most states already support the right of unmarried women to be artificially inseminated, and, in doing so, let them deprive their children of a relationship with their father.

The states do this through deliberate policy. The sperm donor is a "legal stranger" to the child, to use the cold language of the law. If men could be called upon to provide child support, no man would make a deposit in a sperm bank. If women could be required to allow the donor to have a relationship with the child, no woman would make a withdrawal. It is the state's policy of shielding the biological parents from each other that allows anonymous sperm-donor pregnancies to take place.

So who has a natural right to a child, a right that the state should recognize and support? The most compelling candidate is the child's pair of biological parents, who have committed themselves to creating a common life together for the sake of their child as well as themselves. In other words, married couples. They may be said to have a right to a child (though not one that gives them a right to the aid of others or of technologies like artificial insemination), but no one else.

Outsourced Surrogacy Is a Form of Exploitation

Nayantara Mallya

Nayantara Mallya is a writer and a volunteer for SuDatta, an association for adoptive parents.

A couple of years back, a gentleman on an Indian adoptive parents' chat group wrote the following post, "It's better to go for surrogacy as it is guaranteed, unlike adoption. We only have to wait 9 months unlike adoption where the wait maybe 1–2 years. And the child's health and genetics are 100% guaranteed. And the child will be our own." As you can imagine, several adoptive parents replied so furiously that he apologized over and over for his insensitivity.

To me, this guy's attitude was the perfect example of the reasons I condemn professional surrogacy. Because it's about control. And exploitation.

The New Outsourcing

They call it wombs for rent, using a woman's uterus to grow a baby that will be handed over to someone else. First we had BPO [business process outsourcing] then KPO [knowledge process outsourcing], and now reproduction process outsourcing. Foreign couples visit India and return with their 'own' child in their arms—reproductive tourism. India is becoming the surrogacy hub of the world with an estimated Rs. 25,000 crore or more at stake [approx. $5.5 billion]. What a distinctive honour. The experts and the government are hashing out surrogacy laws and guidelines with respect to legalities and the rights of the three concerned parties.

Nayantara Mallya, "Growing the World's Babies in Indian Wombs," *Sa*, November 2, 2009. Reproduced by permission of the author.

Well, why not? Think about it . . . we hire babysitters to take over caring for our kids while we're out at work. We have old age homes or home nurses to take care of our elders. We send the kids to school and tuition teachers to educate them. Outside food is now commonplace with take-aways and eating out happening several times a week. We 'outsource' their medical care to doctors.

A couple who cannot birth a child exploits a woman in a developing country, walks away with a baby in hand, and feels like they helped the surrogate mom get a better life.

Hey, we depend on lots of people to help us bring up our children. So what is wrong with paying a woman to birth our babies, especially a woman who really needs the money? And that too for a couple who really longs for a child?

For one, getting help for child care, education and the care of elders pays people for their skills and work. It's not an invasion of their bodies. Surrogacy is. To me, it compares (in terms of ethics) to paid live organ donation . . . a person's body is being used to save someone else's life. Or commercial sex work . . . a woman is paid to satisfy a man's desires. So a couple who cannot birth a child exploits a woman in a developing country, walks away with baby in hand, and feels like they helped the surrogate mom get a better life. Excuse me?

Without minimizing the anguish and frustration that couples struggling with infertility undergo, I stand clearly against surrogacy. The winners in a successful surrogate arrangement are the genetic parents and the baby that's handed over. The professional surrogate mother also appears to be a winner, with all the money she's paid. But she's not. She's a victim.

Oppression and Exploitation
of the Surrogate

Preferred candidates for surrogacy are married women who have borne one or more healthy children. Like, proof is needed that she can carry a healthy pregnancy—experience on her childbearing career resume. Ridiculous. What are these women's husbands doing? Farming out their wives for child-bearing. To improve their family's quality of life. Thanks to the woman's earnings, the family can afford better housing, education for the kids, a better lifestyle. Excuse me again? This is all wrong.

Anyone who's carried a pregnancy, knows what gestation and birth do to a woman's body and mind. What too many pregnancies and deliveries do to a woman's health, including a long list of complications that can arise from a pregnancy, some minor, some very life-threatening.

It's clear that only 'poor' women take up this option. Women who were probably considered burdens on their parents, married off early to the first willing man, with a concomitant payout of dowry. Followed by a few pregnancies and children. And now a new way to drain the women some more . . . childbearing for payment. And handing over the child to the beaming parents. Wow.

How can women from the so-called developed countries and progressive societies even think about denigrating less fortunate women like this? Other countries have laws that forbid payment for surrogacy. And it's clear that these women would not do this as a free favour. There are plenty of women doing the free favour in families across India; carrying a child for a family member. My husband's friend even considered the option, after 10 years of infertility, but dropped it after my husband explained what one more pregnancy would do to his sister's body. At least he understood.

These hapless women are paid a few lakhs, if the middle-men don't swallow most of it. Some of them carry more than one pregnancy. They get their female relatives also into the 'business'. It's honourable, after all. They're not prostituting, just respectably married women, leasing out their uteri. And the clinics claim the women are counseled and made to understand that they must hand over the baby; that this is only a business arrangement. The women themselves are fooled into believing they've hit on a mega-jackpot.

Surrogacy is the wrong solution to pleasing the patriarchal notions about the requirement for a bloodline produced obediently by the wife and the superiority of genetic ties.

It's a given that a woman from the lower economic classes may not be in the best of health. I say this not from the standpoint of her health's effects on the baby she carries, but the effects on her body. Many surrogacy clinics shelter the pregnant mother during the pregnancy to maintain her privacy and health. While she may receive excellent care during the pregnancy, it's just a matter of good nutrition and rest for a year. After that, she's back to her undernourished and overworked life. Unless of course, she opts to come back for another surrogate pregnancy. So she has to stay pregnant to receive good care, nutrition and money.

The Genetic Parents

Why would anyone make this choice? A couple unable to conceive or carry a full-term pregnancy has so many options available. Where it's possible, medical interventions help conceive miracle babies. Then there's adoption or foster care. Then there's acceptance of a life without children. Some conceive late in life, surprise deliveries of bundles of joy. And now there's the possibility of womb transplants, possibly the first human one could happen within the next two years (although it may come with it's own ethical questions . . . who donates the womb?).

Why do they think their 'own' genes are so important, that they're willing to grow their 'own' baby in someone else's body, but not accept 'someone else's baby' as their own? . . .

Can one actually control a child's health, looks, achievements and future potential simply by ensuring it has our genes? There are no guarantees in life.

Concern for the Surrogate

The biggest concern here should be for the surrogate mom. How does it affect a woman to birth and give away baby after baby? Can baby-growing become a profession? How is she compensated for long-term mental or physical health issues she may develop long after the delivery? Can she go for counseling or therapy if she develops postnatal depression or is unable to emotionally let go of 'her' baby?

Birth mothers who place their children for adoption undergo terrible grief and trauma which can be lifelong. Mothers who suffer neonatal losses will tell you of their anguish and longing for their babies. So how can we assume that a surrogate mother will not feel anything for a child she carried in her body, just because it does not carry her genes? Is that how uncaring we have become?

Why is the Indian government ignoring this abuse of our women's wombs? Surrogacy is the wrong solution to pleasing the patriarchal notions about the requirement for a bloodline produced obediently by the wife and the superiority of genetic ties. It's plain abuse of women, who need to be set free. Instead of empowering poor women to get an education, work and be freed from the shackles of patriarchy, surrogacy enslaves them further. A woman is more than her womb; she's not an unfeeling vessel for breeding. For her to earn money renting out her uterus is a complete blow to women's liberation efforts.

Fertility Doctors Must Consider Children's Well-Being

Thomas H. Murray

Thomas H. Murray is president of the Hastings Center—an independent, nonpartisan, and nonprofit bioethics research institute. He is also a former professor of bioethics at Case Western Reserve University and is the author of The Worth of a Child.

The birth of octuplets to a California woman last week [January 26, 2009] raised a boatload of issues that can distract us from the central ethical question posed by the case: How do we take children's well-being into account in reproductive medicine?

The Parents' and the Child's Interests

Yes, it's puzzling why an unemployed single woman who already had six children wanted a passel more. And it is not crazy to wonder who will pay for these children's needs over the years, beginning with what is sure to be a gobsmacking bill for neonatal intensive care.

For now, we can put aside the lifeboat problem: A human uterus is not built for eight passengers; the odds for each child to be born alive and healthy go down as the number in the lifeboat goes up.

Her physicians offered to reduce the number of fetuses she was carrying; citing her moral convictions, she declined. As of the last reports, all eight survived. Still, knowing what we do about the many risks that come with being born too soon and too small, their medical course is likely to be complex and unsteady.

What this case really does is split wide open a fault line running through infertility treatment in American medicine. People who show up at fertility clinics are adults. In the typical case, they've been trying to get pregnant for a year or more without success.

When all goes well, a cycle of IVF (in vitro fertilization) results in a pregnancy and the birth of one, perhaps two, healthy babies. As a son, a father, and now a grandfather, I can attest that there is no more important or enduring relationship in our lives than the one between parents and children.

Whether that relationship is forged through infertility medicine, adoption or the old-fashioned way matters not at all: What counts is that adults who want to love and raise a child are matched with a child who needs just that love and care.

The ideology of American infertility medicine allows physicians to escape from making any judgments about the suitability of prospective parents.

The point of infertility treatment, after all, is to create a child. But that child-to-be is not the clinic's patient—the would-be parents are. I believe that the interests of those children deserve at least as much consideration as the wishes of the prospective parents.

The Ideology of Infertility Medicine

The vast majority of infertility patients are no doubt fierce advocates for the well-being of the child they so earnestly seek to bring into their lives. What happens, though, when the client's request shows little consideration or regard for the welfare of the would-be children? What happens if a woman in her early 30s with six children wants eight embryos implanted all at once?

A responsible physician could turn down such a request, citing professional guidelines that counsel implanting one, at most two, embryos in women younger than 35. How Nadya Suleman ended up with eight is a mystery. That's what Nadya Suleman is claiming.

Perhaps there is a physician somewhere willing to defy the wisdom of his or her peers; perhaps Suleman used fertility drugs rather than IVF as she claimed. Whatever the case, this guideline is based on safety. Carrying more than a couple of fetuses is dangerous to the pregnant woman and to the health and survival of the fetuses in her womb.

Citing safety is a prudent way to turn down requests an infertility physician thinks are ill-considered. But sometimes that gambit isn't available.

A psychiatrist friend who conducted intake interviews for a well-respected clinic described a rough-looking couple who carried for their up-front payment thousands of dollars in cash stuffed in a bag—drug money, she was certain.

She was able to discourage the couple from following through on their plan. Here's the rub: Her concern was the ultimate well-being of the child that the clinic was being asked to help create. But the ideology of American infertility medicine allows physicians to escape from making any judgments about the suitability of prospective parents.

An Ethical Obligation

There is understandable worry that cracking the door to considerations about parents' motives and capacities would blast it wide open for nasty, petty stereotypes and prejudices. That would be an awful result.

The American Society for Reproductive Medicine acknowledged in a 2004 report that fertility programs may withhold services when they can provide "well-substantiated judgments" that the child will not receive adequate care. But that same report has a huge loophole.

Providers can abdicate almost all responsibility to antici-
pate the welfare of the children they help create by claiming
"an obligation to treat all patients who would benefit from
medical treatment." The statement goes on to say that "except
when significant harm to a future child is likely," they "should
not be required to make assessments of a patient's child-
rearing abilities or other child welfare issues."

It's time for the profession—and business—of reproductive medicine to accept their firm, inescapable ethical obligation to give the interests and well-being of the children they
help to create the same consideration they give to the desires
of the adults they serve.

CHAPTER 4

Is it Ethical for Doctors to End Life?

Overview: End-of-Life Issues

Public Agenda

Public Agenda is a nonpartisan, nonprofit organization that provides research to help American leaders understand the public's view and to help citizens know more about critical policy issues.

The process of dying has become far more complicated than it once was.

A century ago, most people died at home of illnesses that medicine could do little to defeat. Today, a hospital, nursing home or hospice is a far more likely setting, but the place of death is not the only thing that has changed. Technology has created choices for patients and their families—choices that raise basic questions about human dignity and what constitutes a "good death."

Patient Wishes About Death

Most people die in hospitals or institutions where the staff makes a valiant effort to keep patients alive until there is no reasonable chance of recovery. That's exactly what many people want: a no-holds-barred effort to fight off death as long as possible.

For others facing terminal illness, however, there may come a point when the fight no longer seems worth it. Those patients may find their wishes and those of their families overlooked as physicians juggle medical, legal and moral considerations. In most cases, medical professionals have considerable discretion in deciding when additional efforts to sustain life are futile and a patient should be allowed to die.

People face these decisions even before such dire situations come up. Patients undergoing even relatively minor surgical procedures are routinely asked if they would like to fill out a document, known as an "advance directive" or "living will," stating their wishes in the event that they become unable to communicate. Many people choose to prepare living wills in the same way people prepare traditional wills regarding personal property whether they're sick or not.

Court rulings have firmly established a patient's legal right to discontinue life-sustaining treatment, such as respirators or artificial nutrition. There is also extensive precedent for allowing family members to decide whether to continue treatment or end feeding when incapacitated patients are no longer able to decide for themselves.

But the debate over such decisions is far from settled, as was underscored by the 12-year-long legal battle over the fate of Terri Schiavo, who died in 2005 when a court backed her husband's decision to stop feeding her even though her wishes were not in writing.

In most cases, medical professionals have considerable discretion in deciding when additional efforts to sustain life are futile and a patient should be allowed to die.

Another key issue which is unresolved is whether individuals should be able to ask physicians to hasten their deaths—in effect, help them end their lives—and whether it is morally acceptable for physicians to do so.

Fundamental Questions

The debate over "end-of-life issues" is rooted in a number of fundamental questions.

Who decides whether a life is worth living or not? Many people say they would rather die than suffer in great pain or endure life trapped in a vegetative state. Should individuals have the right to decide when and how they will die? Should others—their families, their doctors, the government—be able to decide for them?

What is unbearable? What condition would qualify? Terminal illness? Chronic physical pain? Debilitating, although not fatal, illness? What about severe disabilities?

Is euthanasia—hastening the death of a terminally ill patient—an act of kindness prompted by a sense of mercy and respect for an individual's wishes? Or is it an act of murder and a violation of the Hippocratic Oath?

When physician-assisted suicide is legal, is it a question of giving dying people a measure of control over the timing and manner of their death? Or does it lead to a slippery slope of neglect for the old, the poor, the disabled and those who are emotionally distraught or seriously ill? Could a right to die become a duty to die if the continued life of a patient began to be viewed in terms of the cost for both patients and their families?

What are the religious and moral questions here? For people of many faiths, these decisions touch on deeply held beliefs that life and death should be left to God, not human beings. Others argue that life is something to be cherished and not abandoned, no matter what the circumstances.

Although it is widely condoned around the world, only a handful of nations—the Netherlands, Belgium, Switzerland, and Luxembourg—have made physician-assisted suicide legal.

Are there other alternatives? Advocates of palliative [pain-relieving] care for terminal patients say the real problem is that not enough is done to reduce pain and that patients are not getting enough emotional support. They argue that doctors should be more aggressive in their use of painkillers and do more to address the treatable clinical depression that afflicts many patients.

In the past few decades, especially following Medicare's 1983 addition of some hospice care to its coverage, hospice care has become more common although its availability is poor in many parts of the country.

Physician-Assisted Suicide

Although it is widely condoned around the world, only a handful of nations—the Netherlands, Belgium, Switzerland and Luxembourg—have made physician-assisted suicide legal. In the United States, those who help someone commit suicide may face criminal charges, though laws can vary from state to state. The most famous example is Dr. Jack Kevorkian, who publicly acknowledged helping 130 people commit suicide during the 1990s and served eight years in a Michigan prison for administering a fatal injection to a terminally ill man.

Over the past decade or so, voters in six states have initiated ballot measures to legalize physician-assisted suicide. All except two have failed. In Oregon, voters in 1994 approved the Death with Dignity Act, which permits doctors to prescribe— but not administer—a lethal dose of drugs. The law also established rules to ensure that patients seeking assisted suicide are mentally competent, in great pain and intent on ending their lives. Since the law took effect, about 300 people have committed suicide with the aid of a physician, according to the Oregon Department of Human Services. In Washington [State] this year [2008], voters approved a similar bill.

Initiative measure 1000, the Washington Death with Dignity Act, allows mentally competent, terminally ill adults to request and self-inject a lethal overdose of medication. It unequivocally prohibits euthanasia and lethal injection.

The U.S. Supreme Court has waded into this arena, but the net effect has been to let states decide what to do. In two unanimous 1997 decisions, the high court upheld assisted-suicide bans in New York and Washington states, ruling that terminally ill patients have no constitutional right to medical help in committing suicide. But in 2006, the high court rejected the federal government's effort to block Oregon's law by using its authority to regulate how doctors use prescription drugs.

The Physician's Dilemma

Physicians continue to face a pointed dilemma. "For over 2,000 years, the predominant responsibility of the physician has not been to preserve life at all costs but to serve the patient's needs while respecting the patient's autonomy and dignity," the American Medical Association said in one legal brief. But according to its policy, "physician-assisted suicide is fundamentally incompatible with the physician's role as healer." The Hippocratic Oath, traditionally taken by doctors, states: "To please no one will I prescribe a deadly drug, or give advice which may cause his death."

Every state now allows people to specify in advance, by means of a living will, whether they would want to accept or refuse medical treatment in various circumstances.

A 2007 national poll of doctors points to mixed feelings on the issue of assisted suicide. Fifty-seven percent said it is ethical to assist an individual who has made a rational choice to die due to unbearable suffering; 39 percent said it is unethical. The survey, by the Louis Finkelstein Institute for Religious and Social Studies and HCD Research, found 41 percent of physicians support legalization of assisted suicide in a wide variety of circumstances, 30 percent support legalization only in some cases and 29 percent oppose it without exception.

The numbers are a bit different when doctors are asked whether they personally would assist in a suicide. Forty-six percent said they would not, 34 percent said they would do it in some cases and 20 percent said they would assist in suicide in a wide variety of circumstances. Another key finding: 54 percent believe assisted suicide should be a matter between patient and doctor alone and that government should not regulate the practice. Forty-six percent said the government has a legitimate interest in regulating it.

Deciding in Advance

For a vast majority of people, assisted suicide is not a legal option and even if it were, surveys find large numbers who say they would not consider it. For most, the more relevant question is how to control their medical treatment.

Every state now allows people to specify in advance, by means of a living will, whether they would want to accept or refuse medical treatment in various circumstances. Individuals looking ahead to the possibility that they might not be able to speak for themselves or otherwise communicate can also choose to use a health care proxy to name someone who can make medical decisions on their behalf in such circumstances.

In practice, laws allowing living wills have been limited in their impact. Only about four in ten Americans have advance directives. The wishes outlined in such documents can be difficult to interpret. And many physicians are unaware of their patients' wishes or might be unwilling to implement them. Realistically, if an advance directive has not been discussed and agreed to by family members and doctors, it may not carry much weight.

The Schiavo case, which riveted the nation for weeks in 2005, demonstrated the worst-case scenario in an end-of-life situation: a brain-damaged patient without a written advance directive, a family bitterly divided over what to do, years of litigation and heavy pressure from politicians and advocacy groups.

The courts consistently ruled that Michael Schiavo had the right to remove his wife's feeding tube despite her parents' objections. One consequence of the case was a surge of public interest in living wills. A second effect has been the clarification, by about twenty states, of state laws on advance directives and guardianship for the incapacitated.

A Conflicted Public

This is an intensely personal issue. Surveys show about one-third of Americans say they have had to decide whether to use extraordinary means to keep a loved one alive. About 70 percent of Americans—twice as many as fifty years ago—say doctors should be allowed to help end an incurably ill patient's life when that request is made by the patient and the patient's family.

But polls also show that support falls dramatically when the question is posed in less abstract terms—such as using the phrase "assisted suicide." In a 2007 Gallup poll, for example, 49 percent of Americans said doctor-assisted suicide is morally acceptable; 46 percent disagreed.

There also seems to be a distinction in the public's mind between what they would choose for themselves and what they would choose for others, with far fewer saying they would choose to end treatment for a spouse or child than for themselves. People are divided on whether they would help a terminally ill relative or friend commit suicide to end their suffering.

The public does seem to feel strongly that these are decisions best made by families and doctors, not the government, and most disapproved of Congress's effort to intervene in the Schiavo case.

The Right to Die Necessitates Assistance from Physicians

Jacob M. Appel

Jacob M. Appel is a bioethicist who is a lawyer and holds a medical degree.

Both supporters and opponents of physician-assisted dying anticipated that Judge Dorothy McCarter's groundbreaking ruling that the Montana constitution guaranteed terminally ill, mentally competent adults the right to end their own lives would be appealed to the state's highest court. In her ruling, handed down on December 5, 2008, McCarter wrote that in Montana, the "constitutional rights of individual privacy and human dignity, taken together, encompass the right of a competent terminally ill patient to die with dignity." The plaintiff in that suit, seventy-six-year-old truck driver Robert Baxter of Billings, lost his twelve-year battle with lymphocytic leukemia that same day, without learning of his legal victory.

The Right to Aid in Dying

This week [September 2, 2009], the Montana Supreme Court hears oral arguments in the state's appeal of that seminal verdict. Since the issues arise solely under the state constitution, no further appeals are possible—so a ruling to uphold the lower court's decision will enshrine *Baxter v. Montana* as the case that, for the first time, guarantees the citizens of a state the right to aid in dying. While Oregon's Death with Dignity Act (1994) and Washington's Initiative 1000 [Washington Death with Dignity Act] (2008) grant those states' inhabitants the right to end their own lives, such statutes could be revoked by legislatures at any time. In contrast, a Montana ruling favoring aid in dying would require a constitutional amendment to overturn—an unlikely prospect. However, even a decision to affirm Judge McCarter may prove a Pyrrhic victory [one not worth winning] for supporters of Baxter's cause. As long as no Montana doctors are willing to prescribe lethal medication to patients in need, any "right" to die will offer little palliation [relief] for the ravages of terminal illness.

The right to aid in dying is strikingly useless if nobody is willing to help.

Janet Murdock learned this awful lesson the hard way. The sixty-seven-year-old Missoula woman, who suffered from advanced ovarian cancer, initially believed that Judge McCarter's ruling would guarantee her the death that she desired. Instead, she spent her final months trying to find a local doctor willing to help her die—eventually giving up food and water when no physician in the entire state proved willing to supply her with a lethal dose of medication. Her desperate efforts certainly were not aided by the Montana Medical Association, which issued a policy document declaring aid in dying a violation of professional ethics, or that group's president, Kirk Stoner, who has championed an absolutist, anti-assistance position on the issue. In response, before her death in June, Murdock released a statement that read: "I feel as though my doctors do not feel able to respect my decision to choose aid in dying. . . . Access to physician aid in dying would restore my hope for a peaceful, dignified death in keeping with my values and beliefs." The challenge for those on both sides of this issue is how to balance the "values and beliefs" of desperate patients like Murdock and Baxter with those of medical professionals who are personally opposed to easing their deaths. Our society will soon be forced to adjudicate these competing claims: Which right trumps? The patient's right to die or the doctor's right to follow her conscience?

The Issue of Physician Conscience

The ongoing public debate over "conscience" clauses, which permit individual health care providers to opt out of medical practices to which they are morally opposed, has until now been confined primarily to issues of reproductive freedom. Pharmacists who refuse to fill prescriptions for emergency contraceptives have become lightning rods in the debate over religious freedom and women's health. A critical shortage of abortion providers has led some progressive commentators, including myself, to call for mandatory abortion training in obstetrics residency programs. However, even those policy makers who support conscience exemptions in these areas should be able to recognize the fundamental difference between pharmacists who refuse to fill birth control prescriptions and the physicians who would not help Janet Murdock to die. A handful of rogue druggists may certainly impede access to contraception—but *all* pharmacists do not oppose RU-486 [a drug that induces abortion]. A shortage of abortion providers, while deeply troublesome, is not the same as a complete, statewide absence of abortion providers. If Montana doctors can act on their consciences, patients wishing to die will not merely have to endure additional burdens to vindicate their rights. Rather, they will have absolutely *no* means to effectuate them. Much as constitutional guarantees of press freedom do little good for prospective publishers if they do not have access to paper or ink, the right to aid in dying is strikingly useless if nobody is willing to help.

The state should think creatively about ways to ensure that the terminally ill do not suffer without taking the drastic step of forcing doctors to assist in dying.

The legal profession long ago recognized that if our judicial system is to function meaningfully, all criminal defendants—even the most distasteful—should be entitled to representation. As a result, states provide attorneys for those who cannot find them on their own, and judges occasionally compel individual members of the bar to represent the interests of unpopular defendants. In contrast, doctors have rather stubbornly clung to historic notions of professional autonomy. These arguments might hold more sway if physicians operated in an open marketplace and if anyone with the appropriate knowledge and skills could practice medicine in the United States. In reality, medical licenses are a limited commodity, reflecting an artificial shortage created by a partnership between Congress and organizations representing physicians—with medical school seats and residency positions effectively allotted by the government, much like radio frequencies. Physicians benefit from this arrangement in that a smaller number of physicians inevitably leads to increased rates of reimbursements. There's nothing inherently wrong with this arrangement. However, it belies any claim that doctors should have the same right to choose their customers as barbers or babysitters. Much as the government has been willing to impose duties on radio stations (e.g., indecency codes, equal time rules) that would be impermissible if applied to newspapers, Montana might reasonably consider requiring physicians, in return for the privilege of a medical license, to prescribe medication to the dying without regard to the patient's intent.

Mandating Aid in Dying

Mandating physicians' aid in dying should be a last resort. First, Montana should explore other, less-invasive means of ensuring that all citizens are guaranteed their constitutional right to die. One solution might be hiring a handful of publicly salaried physicians, recruited from out of state, whose primary responsibility would be to offer palliative [pain-relieving] services, including lethal prescriptions, to the terminally ill. Another possibility would be easing licensure requirements for out-of-state physicians, particularly those from

Washington or Oregon, who come to Montana on a short-term basis solely for the purpose of helping the terminally ill to die. Finally, the state might simply scrap its general requirement for physician-issued prescriptions in cases of terminal illness, instead providing both drugs and instructions directly to dying individuals or their families. In short, the state should think creatively about ways to ensure that the terminally ill do not suffer without taking the drastic step of forcing doctors to assist in dying.

The right to die is not an abstract principle. This right—or its absence—has a profound effect on the fundamental welfare of nearly every individual and family in the nation during the most vulnerable moments of their lives. If the Montana Supreme Court guarantees citizens the right to aid in dying, and I am both hopeful and confident that the court will do so, then it is also incumbent upon the justices to ensure a mechanism by which patients can exercise their rights. To do otherwise—to offer a theoretical right to die that cannot be meaningfully exercised—will be both a hollow gesture and a cruel taunt to the terminally ill.

Editor's Note: On December 31, 2009, the Montana Supreme Court ruled that state law protects doctors in Montana from prosecution for helping terminally ill patients die, but failed to go so far as to find a right under the state constitution for physician-assisted suicide.

It Is Ethical for Doctors to Participate in Death Penalty Executions

Dudley Sharp

Dudley Sharp is past vice president and current resource director of Justice for All, a nonprofit criminal justice reform organization working to lessen injury to the innocent and to prosecute the guilty.

Some in the medical community have attempted to create an ethical prohibition against medical professionals' involvement in state executions by invoking the famous "do no harm" credo and the Hippocratic Oath.

It is a dishonest effort. Neither reference is in the context of the state execution of murderers. I find the effort to ban medical professionals' participation in executions an unethical effort to fabricate professional ethical standards, based upon personal anti-death penalty feelings.

The Classical Hippocratic Oath

The select Hippocratic Oath quote, in its original (translated) form, is: "I will neither give a deadly drug to anybody who asked for it, nor will I make a suggestion to this effect. Similarly, I will not give to a woman an abortive remedy. In purity and holiness I will guard my life and my art."

This is a prohibition against euthanasia and abortion and has nothing to do with the fabricated medical prohibition of participation in state sanctioned executions.

I am unaware of any other ancient texts or translations which indicate a historical context, with that quote, that prohibits physicians from participation in executions.

Dudley Sharp, "Physicians & the State Execution of Murderers: No Ethical/Medical Dilemma," HomicideSurvivors.com, October 24, 2009. www.homicidesurvivors.com. Reproduced by permission of the author.

In 2004, Dr. [Howard] Markel, a medical historian, writes, "There are two highly controversial vows in the original Hippocratic Oath that we continue to ponder and struggle with as a profession: the pledges never to participate in euthanasia and abortion."

In reality, these are, barely, controversial, now. They are, however, inconvenient. Dr. Markel's article never mentions a context of state execution of murderers, because the oath has nothing to do with it.

Dr. Markel continues: "The Hippocratics' reasons for refusing to participate in euthanasia may have been based on a philosophical or moral belief in preserving the sanctity of life or simply on their wish to avoid involvement in any act of assisted suicide, murder, or manslaughter."

Dr. Markel is speculating. What we do know is that it was a reference to euthanasia and abortion, specifically. There is not even speculation, by Dr. Markel, that the reference had anything to do with the state execution of murderers.

Various medical associations have fabricated an imagined ethical problem with the death penalty and have, nearly, fully accepted both abortion and euthanasia.

The following are [according to authors Robert Orr and Norman Pang] "the results of a study . . . in which 157 deans of allopathic and osteopathic schools of medicine in Canada and the United States were surveyed regarding the use of the Hippocratic Oath":

1. In 1993, 98% of schools administered some form of the oath.

2. In 1928, only 26% of schools administered some form of the oath.

3. Only 1 school used the original Hippocratic Oath.

4. 68 schools used versions of the original Hippocratic Oath.

5. 100% of current oaths pledge a commitment to patients.

6. Only 43% vow to be accountable for their actions.

7. 14% include a prohibition against euthanasia.

8. Only 11% invoke a diety.

9. 8% prohibit abortion.

10. Only 3% prohibit sexual contact with patients.

There is no mention of the state execution of murderers, because the Hippocratic Oath has nothing to do with it.

The Hypocrisy Oath

Although there is no prohibition on the death penalty, there is one against both euthanasia and abortion. Yet, various medical associations have fabricated an imagined ethical problem with the death penalty and have, nearly, fully accepted both abortion and euthanasia.

Now, only 3% prohibit sexual contact with patients, but the original Hippocratic Oath states: "Whatever houses I may visit, I will come for the benefit of the sick, remaining free of all intentional injustice, of all mischief and in particular of sexual relations with both female and male persons, be they free or slaves."

100% pledge a commitment to their patients, but only 43% vow being accountable for their medical actions. Some commitment. What ethics?

With these survey results and with medical professionals bringing up the Hippocratic Oath, as if it has something to say in the death penalty debate, possibly we should, now, in the true context of euthanasia and abortion, and other issues, call it what it has become, the Hypocrisy Oath.

For example, in January 2007, the North Carolina Medical Board adopted a policy that physicians participating in executions may lose their licenses. In 2009, the North Carolina Supreme Court vacated the board's policy, finding that they had exceeded their authority.

Did the board attempt to prevent physicians from performing abortions or have they issued a statement condemning physicians' participation in euthanasia? Of course not.

The Modern Hippocratic Oath

The modern version is, most often, identified as that penned by Louis Lasagna in 1964.

It states: "It may also be within my power to take a life; this awesome responsibility must be faced with great humbleness and awareness of my own frailty."

This is in the context of killing innocent lives through either abortion or euthanasia.

Quite the about face.

The quote shows physicians' medical ethical/moral acceptance of taking innocent lives.

[According to Markel,] the famous physician credo "'First, do no harm' (a phrase translated into Latin as 'Primum non nocere') is often mistakenly ascribed to the [Hippocratic] Oath, although it appears nowhere in that venerable pledge.

Medical professionals do not violate medical codes of ethics, when participating in the state execution of murderers.

"Hippocrates came closest to issuing this directive in his treatise *Epidemics*, in an axiom that reads, 'As to disease, make a habit of two things—to help, or at least, to do no harm.'"

"As to disease." Nothing else. There is no relevance outside medicine and, most certainly, no prohibition against medical professionals' participation in the state execution of murderers.

Not Medical Treatment

Those ethical codes pertain to the medical profession, only, and to patients, only.

Judicial execution is not part of the medical profession and executions do not make death row inmates patients. Is that news?

The editors of the *PLoS Medicine* [published by the Public Library of Science] agree. They write:

"Execution by lethal injection, even if it uses tools of intensive care such as intravenous tubing and beeping heart monitors, has the same relationship to medicine that an executioner's axe has to surgery."

So too, the American Society of Anesthesiologists: "Although lethal injection mimics certain technical aspects of the practice of anesthesia, capital punishment in any form is not the practice of medicine."

Both confirm the obvious point: The state execution of murderers is not equivalent or connected to the medical treatment of patients. There is no ethical or moral connection. Hardly a mystery.

Any rational person can see that the state execution of murderers is not a medical treatment, but a criminal justice sanction. The basis for medical treatment is to improve the plight of the patient, for which the medical profession provides obvious and daily exceptions. The basis for execution is to carry out a criminal justice sentence where death is the sanction.

Doctors and nurses can be police and soldiers and can kill, when deemed appropriate, within those lines of duty and without violating the ethical codes of their medical profession, because there is no ethical connection. Similarly, medical professionals do not violate medical codes of ethics, when participating in the state execution of murderers.

A Prohibition Based on Bias

Physicians are often part of double- or triple-blind studies where there is hope that the tested drugs may, someday, prove beneficial. The physicians and other researchers know that many patients, taking placebos or less effective drugs, will suffer more additional harm or death because they are not taking the subject drug or that the subject drug will actually harm or kill more patients than the placebo or other drugs used in the study.

Physicians knowingly harm individual patients, in direct contradiction to their "do no harm" oath.

For the greater good, those physicians sacrifice innocent, willing and brave patients. Of course, there have been medical experiments without consent and, even, today, they continue.

Physicians knowingly make exceptions to their "do no harm" requirement, every day, within their profession, where that code actually does apply. And, in many cases, they should. There are obvious ethical nuances and we should consider and pay attention to them, as is done within the medical profession.

Physicians and medical institutions should choose ethical guidelines which are truly relevant to their profession.

Many medical professionals need to stop the ridiculous ethical posturing and tell the truth—they don't like the death penalty. In medical writings against executions, you can easily find a strong bias, evidenced by use of the common and inaccurate anti-death penalty claims, with no apparent effort at fact-checking or balance.

Any participation in executions by medical professionals should be a matter for their own personal conscience. In fact, 20–40% of doctors surveyed would participate in the execution process.

If this physician-created mess had been about long-standing medical ethics, based upon Hippocrates or "do no harm," then there would be an effort to stop medical professionals from participating in euthanasia and abortion. In fact, the opposite has occurred. Instead, irresponsible medical professionals have turned those obvious, historical ethical standards upside down and have fabricated, out of thin air, a prohibition against the death penalty.

Why? For personal reasons, some have decided the formerly unethical medical practices of abortion and euthanasia are, now, just fine and that the nonmedical death penalty is prohibited by a fabricated medical ethic.

There is no foundation for an ethical prohibition against medical professionals participating in executions. Stop using personal bias to fabricate one.

It's unethical.

Doctors Must Respect the Autonomy of Pregnant Women Regarding Abortion

Howard Minkoff and Lynn M. Paltrow

Howard Minkoff is a professor at the State University of New York, Brooklyn, and department chairman of obstetrics and gynecology at the Maimonides Medical Center. Lynn M. Paltrow is the founder and executive director of National Advocates for Pregnant Women, an organization that works to protect the rights and human dignity of all women, particularly pregnant and parenting females.

A quarter century after the "International Year of the Child," we now seem to be in the era of the "Unborn Child." Partly this is because of medical advances: Highly refined imaging techniques have made the fetus more visually accessible to parents. In good measure, however, the new era is a product of political shifts. In 2004, President [George W.] Bush signed into law the Unborn Victims of Violence Act, which makes it a separate federal offense to bring about the death or bodily injury of a "child in utero" while committing certain crimes, and recognizes everything from a zygote to a fetus as an independent "victim" with legal rights distinct from the woman who has been harmed. In 2002, the Department of Health and Human Services adopted new regulations expanding the definition of "child" in the State Children's Health Insurance Program "so that a state may elect to make individuals in the period between conception and birth eligible for coverage." Finally, Senator [Sam] Brownback and thirty-one cosponsors have proposed the Unborn Child Pain Awareness Act [which failed to pass], a scientifically dubious

Howard Minkoff and Lynn M. Paltrow, "The Rights of 'Unborn Children' and the Value of Pregnant Women," *Hastings Center Report*, vol. 36, no. 2, March/April 2006, pp. 26–28. Copyright © 2006 Hastings Center. Reproduced by permission.

piece of legislation that would require physicians performing the exceedingly rare abortions after twenty weeks to inform pregnant women of "the option of choosing to have anesthesia or other pain-reducing drug or drugs administered directly to the pain-capable unborn child."

Fetal Rights and Women's Rights

The legislative focus on the unborn is aimed at women who choose abortion, but it may also have adverse consequences for women who choose not to have an abortion, and it challenges a central tenet of human rights—namely, that no person can be required to submit to state enforced surgery for the benefit of another.

The historical context of fetal rights legislation should make the most fervent proponents of fetal rights—pregnant women—wary. Often, in the past, expansions of fetal rights have been purchased through the diminution of pregnant women's rights. The fetal "right" to protection from environmental toxins cost pregnant women the right to good jobs: For nearly ten years before the U.S. Supreme Court ruled against such polices in 1991, companies used "fetal protection" policies as a basis for prohibiting fertile women from taking high-paying blue collar jobs that might expose them to lead. The fetal "right" to health and life has cost women their bodily integrity (women have been forced to undergo cesarean sections or blood transfusion), their liberty (women have been imprisoned for risking harm to a fetus through alcohol or drug use), and in some cases their lives (a court-ordered cesarean section probably accelerated the death in 1987 of Angela Carder, who had a recurrance of bone cancer that had metastasized to her lung). The fetal "right" not to be exposed to pharmaceutical agents has cost pregnant women their right to participate in drug trials that held out their only hope of cure from lethal illnesses. The vehicle for these infringements on pregnant women's rights has been third parties' assertions that they, rather than the mother, have the authority to speak for the fetus in securing these newly defined rights. For example, employers have argued for the right to speak for the fetus in determining when a work environment is inappropriate for the fetus. In mandating cesarean section, the courts have apparently concluded that the judiciary is better positioned to speak for the fetus and that a competent but dying mother's wishes to refuse surgery are no longer worthy of consideration. Most recently, a state's attorney has taken up the cudgel [a stick or club] for the fetus by charging a woman with murder for her refusal to consent to a cesarean section.

The Unborn Victims of Violence Act

It is within the context of these attempts to wrest the right to speak for the fetus from mothers that legislation that will expand the rights of the fetus—such as the Unborn Victims of Violence Act—must be considered. The act makes the injury or death of a fetus during commission of a crime a federal offense, the punishment for which "is the same as the punishment . . . for that conduct had that injury or death occurred to the unborn child's mother." As written, the law appears unambiguously to immunize pregnant women against legal jeopardy should any act of theirs result in fetal harm: "Nothing in this section shall be construed to permit the prosecution . . . of any woman with respect to her unborn child." But similar statutory guarantees proffered in the past have not been decisive. In 1970 the California legislature created the crime of "fetal murder" and specifically excluded the conduct of the pregnant woman herself, but women who suffered stillbirths were nevertheless prosecuted under the statute. The prosecutor explained that "the fetal murder law was never intended to protect pregnant women from assault by third parties which results in death of the fetus. The purpose was to protect the unborn child from murder."

In Missouri cases, a woman who admitted to smoking marijuana once while pregnant and a pregnant woman who tested positive for cocaine were charged with criminal child endangerment on the basis of a statute that declares the rights of the unborn—yet also includes an explicit exception for the pregnant woman herself in language strikingly similar to that used in the Unborn Victims [of Violence] Act ("nothing in this section shall be interpreted as creating a cause of action against a woman for indirectly harming her unborn child by failing to properly care for herself"). The state argued that this language did not preclude prosecution of the pregnant women because "the pregnant woman is not in a different position than a third party who injures the unborn child" and because her drug use "'directly' endangered the unborn child."

No person can be required to submit to state enforced surgery for the benefit of another.

The Erosion of Women's Rights

Even if the historical record did not contain these examples of a legislative bait and switch, the principles codified by the new federal statute would be worrisome. When laws create parity between harming pregnant women and harming members "of the species Homo sapiens" of any gestational age (as the Unborn Victims of Violence Act specifies), they establish symmetry between the rights of pregnant women and those of fetuses. In so doing, they suggest a need to balance rights when those rights appear to conflict with each other, and potentially to subordinate the rights of the women to those of the fetus. But to take this stance is not merely to elevate the rights of the unborn to parity with those of born individuals. It is in fact to grant them rights previously denied to born individuals: Courts have allowed forced surgery to benefit the unborn, but have precluded forced surgery to benefit born persons. In

1978 Robert McFall sought a court order to force his cousin David Shimp, the only known compatible donor, to submit to a transplant. The court declined, explaining: "For our law to compel the defendant to submit to an intrusion of his body would change every concept and principle upon which our society is founded. To do so would defeat the sanctity of the individual and would impose a rule which would know no limits."

The Unborn Child Pain Awareness Act is yet another example of a law focused on the fetus that devalues pregnant women and children and sets the stage for further erosion of their human rights. It mandates that prior to elective terminations, physicians deliver a precisely worded, though scientifically questionable, monologue that details the purported pain felt by the fetus and allows for fetal pain management. In so doing, it introduces two damaging concepts. First, it makes women and abortion providers a unique class, excluded from the standard medical model in which counseling is provided by a physician who uses professional judgment to determine what a reasonable individual would need in order to make an informed choice about a procedure. Instead, legislators' judgment is substituted for a physician's determination of the appropriate content of counseling.

Second, it elevates the rights of the mid-trimester fetus beyond those of term fetuses, as well as those of its born siblings. Congress has never mandated that mothers be told that there may be fetal pain associated with fetal scalp electrodes or forceps deliveries. Nor have doctors been compelled to speak of the pain that accompanies circumcision or, for that matter, numerous medical conditions for which people are prevented from receiving adequate palliative [pain-relieving] care. Indeed, there is no federal law scripting counseling about the pain that could accompany any procedure to any child, or indeed any person, after birth. Society has generally relied on professionals to exercise medical judgment in crafting the content of counseling, and on medical societies to assure that counseling evolves as science progresses.

While support for fetal rights laws is now *de rigueur* [necessary] among politicians, there is apparently no similar mandate to address the social issues that truly threaten pregnant women and victimize their fetuses. Although states increasingly are seeking ways to arrest and punish women who won't undergo recommended surgery or who are unable to find drug rehabilitation programs that properly treat pregnant women and families, no means have been found to guarantee paid maternity leave or to proffer more than quite limited employment protections from discrimination for women when they are pregnant. Many of our nation's tax and social security policies, rather than bolstering women's social standing, help to ensure mothers' economic vulnerability. Hence, the opposition to the Unborn Victims of Violence Act from some activists must be recognized as the logical consequence of years of having mothers beatified in words and vilified in deeds.

The Responsibility of Physicians

These arguments should not be misconstrued as evidence of a "maternal-fetal" conflict. Unless stripped of their rights, pregnant women will continue to be the most powerful advocates for the well-being of unborn children. Clashes between the rights of mothers and their fetuses are used as Trojan horses by those who would undermine the protections written into law by *Roe* [*v. Wade* (1973)] Proponents of the right-to-life agenda recognize that when fetal rights expand, the right to abortion will inevitably contract. Furthermore, the responsibilities of physicians in this environment are clear and are grounded in the principles of professionalism—primacy of patient welfare, patient autonomy, and social justice. Those principles require that patients' needs be placed before any "societal pressures" and that "patients' decisions about their care must be paramount." These words are bright line guideposts for clinicians who may at times feel caught in a balancing act. Whether the counterclaim to a pregnant woman's right to autonomy is a societal demand for drug test results obtained in labor, an administrator's request to get a court order to supersede an informed woman's choice, or a colleague's plea to consider fetal interests more forcefully, these principles remind us that no other concern should dilute physicians' commitment to the pregnant woman.

The Unborn Child Pain Awareness Act is yet another example of a law focused on the fetus that devalues pregnant women and children.

The argument that women should not lose their civil and human rights upon becoming pregnant is predicated neither on the denial of the concept that an obstetrician has two patients, nor on the acceptance of any set position in the insoluble debate as to when life begins. The courts have provided direction for those dealing with the competing interests of two patients, even if one were to concede that the fetus in this regard is vested with rights equal to that of a born person. A physician who had both Robert McFall (potential marrow recipient) and David Shimp (potential donor) as patients may well have shared the judge's belief that Shimp's refusal to donate his marrow, and thereby to condemn McFall to death, was "morally reprehensible." But the clinician would ultimately have to be guided by the judge's decision to vouchsafe David Shimp's sanctity as an individual. Pregnancy does not diminish that sanctity or elevate the rights of the fetus beyond that of Robert McFall or any other born person. Thus, while the obstetrician's commitment to his "other" patient (the fetus) should be unstinting, it should be so only to a limit set by those, to quote Justice [Harry] Blackmun, "who conceive, bear, support, and raise them." To do otherwise would be to

161

recruit the medical community into complicity with those who would erode the rights of women in the misguided belief that one can champion the health of children by devaluing the rights of their mothers.

Doctors and Nurses Should Never Take Part in Euthanasia

Jean Echlin

Jean Echlin is a nursing consultant in palliative care and advisor to the deVeber Institute for Bioethics and Social Research, a Canadian organization that conducts research on topics connected to human life in its biological, social, and ethical dimensions.

A deadly and distorted ideology is aggressively seeking to take hold in our culture. It calls itself *Compassion & Choices* or *Death with Dignity* or other similar names. Its leaders and adherents support and promote euthanasia and assisted suicide, which they call "aid-in-dying." This movement's leaders insist that physicians, nurses or other health care providers prescribe and give lethal injections, or the gas, or the drugs necessary to kill a person, or for persons to kill themselves.

Professional health care relationships—among doctors, nurses, patients and family members—are based on trust. Asking professional health care providers to kill, or give the means to kill, will destroy this trust relationship. We should never ask our professional caregivers to provide us with the means of our death. Neither should our health care providers ever feel bound to comply with this request.

The Danger of a Duty to Die

Currently, several million dollars are being collected throughout the U.S. to assist proponents of I-1000 [Initiative 1000, Washington Death with Dignity Act] that would legalize assisted suicide in Washington State [passed November 4, 2008]. Unfortunately, many people in our culture have very little un-

Jean Echlin, "Death with Dignity or Obscenity?" deVeber Institute for Bioethics and Social Research, October 28, 2008. Reproduced by permission.

derstanding of what this will mean in their future, in the future of their parents and the future of their children. Why are these dollars not being used to promote good pain management and excellence in end-of-life care?

By voting for the legalization of euthanasia and assisted suicide, you will help to authorize, potentially, the death of yourself and/or family members regardless of age or ability to consent.

Take, for example, your 78-year-old mother who has been devastated and feels very depressed following the death of her spouse of more than 50 years. In addition, she has a treatable but possibly late-stage illness. How will you respond? Is it not in your mother's best interest to get counseling in an attempt to treat her depression? If she were to call upon an advocate of *Compassion & Choices* or *Death with Dignity*, she would likely be encouraged to take the quick and easy way out. An estimated 73% of all assisted-suicide deaths in the state of Oregon, the only American state where assisted suicide is legal [joined by Washington in 2008 and Montana in 2010], are facilitated in some manner by *Compassion & Choices*. When the "Right to Die" lobby and the end-of-life decision maker are the same people, there is no protection for your vulnerable mother.

It is easy to see that legal assisted suicide can quickly become coercion to die and "duty to die."

Consider the real-life situation of a 54-year-old Oregon woman named Barbara Wagner. She was denied effective treatment for lung cancer but offered assisted suicide by the Oregon Department of Health.

What would you do in this situation? Could you afford to pay for the chemotherapy to assist her self-determination to live longer?

It is easy to see that legal assisted suicide can quickly become coercion to die and "duty to die."

Death Is Not the Solution

The disciples of the cult of euthanasia and assisted suicide would have society believe that the logical solution for pain and suffering is death. They may even see the infliction of death or the provision of assisted suicide as part of hospice palliative [pain-relieving] care. They pursue with missionary zeal their gospel of death. Further, they often succeed in getting mainstream media to support their cause.

Those medical professionals and organizations who practice or support euthanasia and assisted suicide as "mercy killing" should not be involved in hospice palliative care. In addition, they should not sit on governing bodies, advisory councils, or committees that develop standards of practice for palliative care. This may mean that parallel programs not inclusive of assisted suicide and euthanasia may need to be developed.

If the law is changed to allow euthanasia and assisted suicide, those at highest risk will be:

- Older women (55 and above) or elderly fragile men

- Individuals with physical or mental disabilities

- Partners in scenarios of domestic violence

- Babies and children born with disabilities and birth anomalies

- Persons who are poor and disenfranchised

- Members of minority groups

A Particular Concern for Women

Derek Humphry, cofounder of the Hemlock Society, put his notion of "self-deliverance" into practice in the death of his first wife, Jean. He and second wife Ann wrote *Jean's Way*, the book that helped him rise to power and prestige in the cult of death. Later, he participated, with Ann's help, in procuring the death of Ann's parents—something she came to bitterly regret.

When Ann developed cancer, Derek responded by encouraging her to end her life. When she decided to seek treatment, he left her. But eventually she took her life.

Her last words to Derek include the following: "*What you did—desertion and abandonment and subsequent harassment of a dying woman—is so unspeakable there are no words to describe the horror of it.*"

This leads to the question, does assisted death really have anything to do with love and compassion or is it often a misogynistic [characterized by a hatred toward women] act?

Historically, women have been vulnerable to male authority in politics, law, government, religion and medicine.

Researchers [J.E.] Malphurs and [D.] Cohen published their findings in, *A Statewide Case-Control Study of Spousal Homicide-Suicide in Older Persons*. They studied twenty cases of homicide-suicide conducted over a two-year period in the state of Florida. Their interest was not in euthanasia or assisted suicide, but mental health issues around suicide and homicide. Their study was published in the *American Journal of Geriatric Psychiatry*.

They found that 25% of homicide-suicide perpetrators had a history of domestic violence. In the study, all of the perpetrators were men and 40% were caregivers for their wives. Furthermore, they noted that 65% of homicide-suicide perpetrators and 80% of suicides where a man committed suicide alone were men who were depressed. All the perpetrators in this study were men who were described as dominating, controlling individuals. The research points out that "depression" is prominent in persons of all ages who commit suicide. It also points out that most often the husband is the perpetrator and the wife is the victim.

The cases of Tracy Latimer in Saskatchewan and Terri Schiavo in Florida follow a similar story line.

The State of Oregon

The Oregon Death with Dignity Act took effect in 1997. Data collected in that state reveal the flaws in the legislation. According to researchers [Herbert] Hendin and [Kathleen] Foley, safeguards for the care and protection of terminally ill patients under this law are being circumvented. One of the key problems seems to be the lack of appropriate data collected by the Oregon Public Health Division (OPHD) who is charged with monitoring the law. This organization failed to "ensure that palliative care alternatives to physician-assisted suicide (PAS) are made available to patients" and they also failed to protect vulnerable patients by not ensuring that the safeguards are upheld.

This study further points out that "the unintended consequences of (a single criterion of six months or less to live) is that it enables physicians to assist with suicide without inquiring into the source of the medical, psychological, social and existential concerns that usually underlie the requests for assisted suicide, even though this type of inquiry produces the kind of discussion that often leads to relief for patients and makes assisted suicide seem unnecessary."

The editorial board for Oregon's largest newspaper, the *Oregonian*, opposes Washington State's I-1000 initiative. They wrote, "Don't go there! We won't be endorsing it. Our fundamental objection is the same as it's always been—that it's wrong to use physicians and pharmacists to hasten patients' deaths."

They also point to lack of transparency in the Oregon experience: "Oregon's physician-assisted suicide program has not been sufficiently transparent. Essentially, a coterie of insiders run the program, with a handful of doctors and others deciding what the public may know. We're aware of no substantiated abuses, but we'd feel more confident with more sunlight on the program."

Physicians are not required to be knowledgeable about the relief of physical and emotional pain and suffering. This situation is shocking and should be unacceptable under the law. Oregon's Death with Dignity Act protects doctors much more than patients.

The Netherlands

Of interest are the Dutch government reports about euthanasia and physician-assisted suicide. The 1990, 1995, and 2001 reports are horrifying. In addition, a study published in the *New England Journal of Medicine* entitled: "End-of-Life Practices in the Netherlands Under the Euthanasia Act" states: "in 2005 there were

- 2,325 euthanasia deaths;

- approximately 100 assisted-suicide deaths; and

- approximately 9,685 deaths related to terminal sedation.

- 550 deaths without request were reported".

In the previous Dutch reports these deaths without permission or request were in the range of 1,000 persons per year. These deaths are often imposed by physicians without the knowledge of the patient or family.

The numbers in the Dutch studies *do not include* the euthanasia deaths of handicapped infants and children or children up to the age of 12 with life-threatening illnesses. This takes place under the recent Groningen Protocol.

The studies *do include* patients with mental health/psychiatric problems. Such persons may be cognitively impaired and unable to understand the consequences of their decisions.

Earlier Dutch reports indicated that doctors deliberately killed approximately 11,800 people each year by euthanasia, assisted suicide, or other intentional actions or explicit omissions. The most recent reports would indicate that these numbers have increased.

As noted by Alex Schadenberg, chair of the Euthanasia Prevention Coalition (International), the decreased incidence of active euthanasia is directly related to the incredible increase in deaths by terminal sedation in the Netherlands.

Euthanasia is out of control in the Netherlands. People have good reason to be afraid of going into acute care or long-term care institutions. Some people carry a card stating their wish not to be euthanized.

This is unconscionable in terms of medical practice. The word "obscenity" in dying comes to mind.

Dangers with Legalization of Euthanasia

The legalization of euthanasia would remove a patient's autonomy and put it into the hands of professionals with potential control issues; who may be angry, sadistic and abusive. We have all seen colleagues both at the bedside and in health care management who have significant personality flaws, and, lacking compassion for the pain and suffering of others, feel they can take the law into their own hands.

Doctors and nurses should never be killers.

The doctors in Nazi-led Germany who experimented with various methods of killing people with disabilities (mental or physical) under the eugenic ideology will be replaced by doctors and nurses who are willing to take part in the deadly evil called euthanasia and assisted suicide.

Everyone should be concerned by the possibilities of euthanasia and assisted suicide changing the value and dignity that is attributed to the dying, chronically ill and people with disabilities. This is especially true in health care systems facing financial and resource cutbacks where death may be seen as more fiscally efficacious than life.

A 1998 study from Georgetown University's Center for Clinical Bioethics found a strong link between cost-cutting pressures on physicians and their willingness to prescribe lethal drugs to patients—were it legal to do so.

Doctors and nurses should never be killers.

The Palliative Care Alternative

Hospice palliative care is the provision of pain and symptom management for individuals experiencing life-threatening, life-limiting, progressive, or terminal disease. The cornerstone of excellence in this newer health care reform is the management of pain and other distressing symptoms. A person in pain is unable to focus on anything except his need for pain relief. Having to cry or plead for pain or anxiety medication leaves the patient feeling degraded, demoralized and dehumanized. In cases like these, their desperation is often distressing enough to make them wish for death. Individuals have the right to appropriate pain and symptom management.

The intention is to relieve pain and suffering, not to hasten death.

In addition, palliative care focuses on emotional, social and existential suffering. This care may be combined with therapies aimed at reducing or curing the illness or it may be the total focus of care. Grief and bereavement follow-up may be a part of this caring process.

Many therapeutic modes exist to help with the pain experience. These include, but are not limited to, the use of narcotics, nerve blocks, surgery, radiation, chemotherapy, guided imagery and relaxation techniques, therapeutic touch, reiki [palm healing], hypnosis, music and art therapy.

Programs of hospice palliative care take a multidisciplinary team approach utilizing the skills of doctors, nurses, chaplains, social workers and physiotherapists, with the added benefit of trained volunteers.

Including these in the care of patient and family can provide enough quality end-of-life support to eliminate the desire for a premature death caused by euthanasia or assisted suicide. For the infrequent situations where pain and anxiety may appear unmanageable, "palliative sedation" may be considered. This is not euthanasia. It is good palliative care. The intention is to relieve pain and suffering, not to hasten death.

Palliative Sedation and Terminal Sedation

It is important to note that there is a difference between "palliative sedation" and "terminal sedation." Unfortunately the literature does not recognize this.

Palliative sedation is medication given to relieve the distress of a terminally ill patient in his last hours or days when other methods of pain management have failed the patient. This only happens in a low percentage of patients—approximately 2 to 5 percent who have a pain escalation/surge at the very end of life. According to the *Journal of Hospice and Palliative Nursing*, in the article "The Process of Palliative Sedation" four criteria should be present:

- Symptoms that are unbearable and unmanageable

- A current do not resuscitate order (DNR) must be in effect

- A terminal diagnosis

- Death must be imminent within hours to days

It would be helpful to have a separate consent for palliative sedation. This would avoid any confusion around treatment plans. The intent of palliative sedation is to provide pain and symptom relief and not to hasten death.

On the other hand, "terminal sedation" as it is practiced in the Netherlands appears to be sedation followed by dehydration with the explicit intention of causing death.

One of the most significant findings in current literature indicates that the use of opiates (morphine, hydromorphone, fentanyl, etc.) when properly titrated according to the patient's pain intensity, do not hasten death. Also, this is one reason narcotics are not the drugs of choice for euthanasia or assisted suicide.

One of the most difficult clinical assessments is the determination of when a human being is actually "terminal." A disease can be labeled terminal at diagnosis, as in terminal cancer. This does not mean that a person is imminently dying. In fact, the life span may be anywhere from months to years. It is often difficult for the most astute diagnostician to predict the actual end stage or terminal stage of disease. This is true of the major categories of disease such as cardiovascular, neurological, cancer, renal failure, diabetes, etc.

How dare we assume that a diagnosis of a life-threatening illness means that a person is "terminal?" One significant lesson learned from the bedside of a patient of mine is: "Do not let anyone label me 'terminal.' I will tell you when it is my time. Give me a measure of hope and speak to my living!" These were the words spoken by a 38-year-old man who desperately wanted to live.

Individuals facing life-threatening disease are usually depressed. Depression is treatable even in late-stage disease. Thus, euthanasia and assisted suicide represent a threat to people both needing medical and psychological support for clinical depression.

Dying Without Pain

Everybody needs to have access to quality end-of-life care through hospice palliative care programs. Further, medical practitioners, nurses, pharmacists and other members of the health care team should keep informed of newer methods of pain and symptom management. This should be a mandatory requirement through the various licensing bodies.

Palliative care is a life-giving therapy, not a life-limiting therapy.

According to Dr. M. Scott Peck in his book, *Denial of the Soul: Spiritual and Medical Perspectives on Euthanasia and Mortality*: "Failure to treat pain is medical malpractice . . . it is one of the worst crimes in medicine today." His words ring true and he too suffered the pain experience.

Today, there is no excuse for any individual, be they adult or infant, to experience an agonizing death. We have an armamentarium of methods and pharmaceuticals (medications) to modify physical pain and death anxiety. Unfortunately, too many of our health care providers, particularly nurses and doctors, are not effectively trained in the principles and practices of this newer health care reform (30 years) called hospice palliative care. Neither are they educated in the newer methods of pain relief for acute, chronic and end-stage disease.

In my 29 years as a palliative care nurse consultant, I have been at the bedside of more than 1,000 dying individuals. It is my learned experience that persons who receive timely, appropriate and expert pain and symptom management, including attention to their significant issues, do not ask for assisted suicide or euthanasia. According to Dr. Neil MacDonald in the *Palliative Medicine: A Case-Based Manual*, proper pain management can actually extend the life span as patients experience improved quality of life. Palliative care is a life-giving therapy, not a life-limiting therapy. Dying with dignity can only be achieved with expert hospice palliative care. This is the compassionate choice and should be available for every individual in Canada and the United States, throughout their life span. Expert hospice palliative care requires a commitment of health care dollars, strong community and institutional and home health care and compassionate support for vulnerable people.

There Is No Humane Way of Performing Death Penalty Executions

PLoS Medicine Editors

PLoS Medicine is a medical journal providing a venue for research and comment on the major challenges to human health worldwide, and its editors have expertise in the fields of medicine, health sciences, and ethics.

This month's issue [April 2007] of *PLoS Medicine* contains a research article on three protocols used in lethal injection, the current method of execution for most US states. Despite the British Royal Commission on Capital Punishment advising against lethal injection half a century ago, the United Nations General Assembly affirming the desirability of abolishing the death penalty in 1971, and the European Union explicitly banning the death penalty in all circumstances, execution—predominantly by lethal injection—is still practiced in many countries. During 2005 at least 2,148 people were executed in 22 countries in cases recorded by Amnesty International; the actual numbers were certainly higher. The majority of these executions took place in China, where fleets of mobile execution vans have been deployed to facilitate prompt, low-profile executions by lethal injection. Iran, Saudi Arabia, and the US [United States] together with China accounted for 94% of executions in 2005.

Execution by Lethal Injection

Following its introduction to the US in 1982, lethal injection became the primary method of execution there, largely replacing execution by hanging, firing squad, gas chamber, and elec-

"Lethal Injection Is Not Humane," *PLoS Medicine*, vol. 4, no. 4, April 2007, pp. 603–604. Copyright © 2007 The PLoS Medicine Editors. Reproduced by permission.

trocution. Each of these older methods has come to be seen as inhumane or excessively violent by most states, but each remains an option in a handful of others. Of the 53 executions in the US in 2006, all but one (an electrocution) were carried out using lethal injection.

In recent months, concerns over botched lethal injections have put the method on hold in a dozen or so of the 36 US states that have the death penalty. Following a particularly agonizing execution in December 2006, the US District Court ruled that California's lethal injection protocol was unconstitutional. The governors of Florida and Tennessee suspended executions pending review of their states' lethal injection protocols. A court ruling in December 2006 suspended Maryland's executions, and New Jersey is considering an outright ban on its death penalty following a 2004 court order requiring the state to justify its lethal injection process. Executions are on hold in several other states pending legal proceedings.

In this context, the editors of *PLoS Medicine* believe it is timely to publish a research article reporting shortcomings of lethal injection protocols. Strictly speaking, this article has little to do with medicine. Execution by lethal injection, even if it uses tools of intensive care such as intravenous tubing and beeping heart monitors, has the same relationship to medicine that an executioner's axe has to surgery. Nonetheless, there is a need for greater openness in public discussion and consideration of the death penalty, including its unpalatable details.

No Human Execution

Challenges to the constitutionality of lethal injection have thus far been based largely on accounts of suffering resulting from unskilled administration. The American Medical Association, the American Nurses Association, the Society of Correctional Physicians, and a number of state medical boards have banned as unethical any causative role for medical professionals in executions. Accordingly, in lethal injection procedures intravenous access has often been attempted (with frequent failures) by untrained staff, the execution mixture has precipitated and blocked IV [intravenous] tubes, and lethal doses have been unreliably calculated. Anesthesia has failed, chemical burns have occurred, and suffering has proceeded for 30 minutes or longer. Although this suffering might be seen as a consequence of professional refusal to participate in executions, this refusal also appears to be one of the primary forces motivating reexamination of lethal injection by the courts.

It is time for the US to join the majority of countries worldwide in recognizing that there is no humane way of forcibly killing someone.

The current article by [Leonidas G.] Koniaris and colleagues gives further cause for concern by questioning whether, even if "perfectly" administered, the protocols would achieve their stated aim of causing death without inflicting inhumane punishment. The authors analyzed several cases from three states: California, North Carolina, and Virginia. (Texas, the state with the largest number of lethal injections, does not release data from executions.) These lethal injection protocols use the barbiturate thiopental (intended to sedate and to suppress breathing), the neuromuscular blocker pancuronium (which paralyzes, causing respiratory arrest, but also preventing agonal movements that might indicate suffering), and the electrolyte potassium (intended to cause cardiac arrest). Such protocols are intended to provide redundancy, such that each drug is given at a dose that would by itself cause death. However, in analyzing data from actual executions, Koniaris and colleagues report that thiopental and potassium do not consistently result in death. In fact, individuals undergoing execution have continued to breathe after the injection of thiopental, and their hearts have continued to beat following injection of potassium; in these cases, the authors conclude, it is quite likely that those being executed have experienced asphyxiation while conscious and unable to move, and possibly an intense burning pain throughout the body from the potassium injection.

Each of the editors of *PLoS Medicine* opposes the death penalty. It is not our intention to encourage further research to "improve" lethal injection protocols. As editors of a medical journal, we must ensure that research is ethical, and there is no ethical way to establish the humaneness of procedures for killing people who do not wish to die. Human research to further the ends of governments at the expense of individual lives is an obvious violation of the Declaration of Helsinki, which was conceived largely in response to the atrocities of Nazi "medicine" in order to articulate an international standard for ethical human experimentation. Whatever local law might say in a given place and time, no ethical researcher would propose a study to establish such procedures, no ethical reviewers would approve it, and no ethical journal would publish it. The acceptability of lethal injection under the US Constitution's Eighth Amendment ban on inhumane punishment has never been established; the data presented by Koniaris and colleagues adds to the evidence that lethal injection is simply the latest in a long line of execution methods that have been found to be inhumane. It is time for the US to join the majority of countries worldwide in recognizing that there is no humane way of forcibly killing someone.

The Accuracy of Convictions

Apart from the issue of whether humane execution can exist, we must also consider the accuracy of convictions resulting in death sentences. Execution of wrongfully sentenced individuals is obviously unacceptable, yet between 1973 and 2004 in the US, 118 prisoners who had been sentenced to death were later released on grounds of innocence. Of 197 convictions in the US that were subsequently exonerated by DNA evidence, 14 were at one time sentenced to death or served time on death row. Racial bias in sentencing likely accounts for much of this error; more than half of the exonerees were African Americans, and the rate of death sentences in the US among those convicted of killing a white victim is considerably higher than for murderers of blacks. Given this potential for fatal error, how can any objective person support the death penalty, which allows for no correction?

Physicians and nurses are saying that their involvement in executions is below any acceptable conception of professional ethics.

We support the recent decision of Craig Watkins, the new district attorney of Dallas, Texas, to examine hundreds of cases over the past 30 years to see whether DNA tests might reveal wrongful convictions. Such errors are inevitable when an implicit goal of sentencing, and particularly of imposing the death penalty, is not rational but emotional: the desire for revenge. As one law professor [Elizabeth Weil] stated in a recent *New York Times Magazine* article on lethal injection, "Retribution, the conscious affliction of pain and suffering because and only because some people deserve it, is the essence of punishment." But if the personal satisfaction of seeing criminals "get what they deserve" really reflects the intentions of Americans, why has the US seen a transition away from firing squad, hanging, or even drawing and quartering? Why was capital punishment illegal for a decade until it was reinstated by a Supreme Court ruling in 1976? Why have some US states rejected the death penalty completely, and others suspended its use? Why has the US followed the course associated with totalitarian states and rejected by other democracies in this matter?

Clearly, the death penalty is a matter of profound ambivalence in American society. Courts and state governments are saying that if capital punishment exists, it must not be cruel or visibly violent. Physicians and nurses are saying that their involvement in executions is below any acceptable conception of professional ethics. How to reconcile the needs of a society given to vengeance but outwardly abhorrent of cruelty or violence, trusting of medical science's trappings but indifferent to their use in killing, expecting the highest ethics of its physicians but willing to medicalize the execution chamber? The new data in *PLoS Medicine* will further strengthen the constitutional case for the abandonment of execution in the US. As a moral society, the US should take a leading role in the abandonment of executions worldwide.

It Is Ethical for Doctors to Refuse to Perform Abortion

Daniel Allott and Matt Bowman

Daniel Allott is a policy analyst at American Values, a public policy organization in Washington, D.C. Matt Bowman is a constitutional law attorney and a contributor to the blog at CatholicVote.org.

Nurse Catherina Cenzon-DeCarlo winced as the doctor inserted forceps into his patient's dilated cervix and pushed them deep into her uterus. Then she stood shocked as he carefully plucked, piece by piece, parts of the patient's unborn child, pulling them back through the cervix and vagina, and ultimately placed them in a specimen cup. DeCarlo then was required to pour saline into the cup and deliver the bloody body parts to the specimen room.

A Nurse's Struggle of Conscience

On May 24 [2009], DeCarlo, a nurse at Mount Sinai Medical Center in New York City, was forced to participate in the killing of a 22-week-old unborn child by dismemberment. As she began her shift that morning, a superior informed her that she needed to assist in the late second-term abortion. DeCarlo protested that as a practicing Catholic, she had strongly held religious beliefs against killing unborn children.

Though she had repeatedly and in writing made her belief known to hospital administrators since she was hired five years earlier, DeCarlo was told on that day that if she did not participate, she would be charged with "insubordination and patient abandonment." That meant she might lose her job or her nursing license or both. Despite repeated tearful pleas, De-

Daniel Allott and Matt Bowman, "The Right of Conscience in the Age of Obama: It Can No Longer Be Taken for Granted," *American Spectator*, vol. 42, no. 9, November 2009, pp. 22–27. Copyright © The American Spectator 2009, Reproduced by permission.

Carlo was refused. The next day, DeCarlo called the Alliance Defense Fund, which has filed a federal lawsuit on her behalf. DeCarlo stated later:

> I couldn't believe that this could happen in the United States, where freedom is held sacred. I still remember the baby's mangled body with twisted and torn arms, fingers, legs and feet. It felt like a horror film unfolding. I kept imagining the pain this baby must have gone through while being torn apart with the forceps. It was devastating.

Pro-life advocates have had a year to come to terms with the most strident abortion advocate ever to ascend to the U.S. presidency. Having relied on either a pro-life president or pro-life congressional majority for 26 of the last 29 years, they confront an opposition emboldened as never before.

Despite the vast body of laws protecting conscience rights, there have been numerous recent attempts to weaken them through legislation.

Nowhere is the scope of the abortion movement's ambition more evident than in its aggressive attacks on the rights of health care providers not to participate in life-destroying procedures. Through their statements and actions, Barack Obama and his abortion industry allies are pushing their goal to make experiences like DeCarlo's much more common.

Conscience Rights

The primacy of conscience is well established in American law. In 1973, after the U.S. Supreme Court's *Roe v. Wade* decision legalizing abortion nationwide, Congress passed the Church Amendment, which exempts private entities that receive public funds from having to provide abortions or sterilizations, and protects health care workers from being forced to assist in abortions and other practices if they work for fund recipients.

Subsequent laws have reinforced federal conscience rights and extended them to prohibit discrimination at all levels of government for refusing to participate in or train for abortion. According to the Guttmacher Institute, a nonprofit research organization affiliated with Planned Parenthood, 46 states also allow some health care providers to refuse involvement in abortion.

Despite the vast body of laws protecting conscience rights, there have been numerous recent attempts to weaken them through legislation, the courts, and licensing boards. In 1995, the Accreditation Council for Graduate Medical Education passed a regulation to mandate abortion training for medical school accreditation, and only federal law prevented its enforcement.

In 1997, the Alaska Supreme Court ordered a private, non-sectarian, pro-life hospital to begin performing abortions. And over the past decade, New York, Massachusetts, and California have considered laws to force private hospitals to provide abortion and other services.

Doctors and Nurses Under Pressure

Perhaps the most consequential blow to conscience rights came in the form of a simple statement. In November 2007, the American College of Obstetricians and Gynecologists (ACOG) declared that health care providers may not exercise their right of conscience if it might "constitute an imposition of religious or moral beliefs on patients."

Shortly thereafter, the American Board of Obstetrics and Gynecology (ABOG) issued a policy stating that board certification can be revoked "if there is a violation of ABOG or ACOG rules and or ethics principles or felony convictions."

According to Donna Harrison, MD, president of the American Association of Pro-Life Obstetricians and Gynecologists, the ACOG-ABOG policy would drive all pro-life ob/gyns out of practice. "In order to practice in hospitals you have to have board certification," she said in an interview. "Obstetricians and gynecologists have to practice in hospitals because they are procedure-surgery based. If you can't get hospital privileges, you can't practice."

Michael Leavitt, secretary of health and human services under President George W. Bush, summed up the medical establishment's position: "[I]f a person goes to medical school, they lose their right of conscience."

Conscience violations have become common. Freedom2-Care, a coalition of 46 groups organized by the Christian Medical Association (CMA), lists on its Web site more than 50 instances of discrimination against secretaries, physicians, pharmacists, and hospitals. The number is likely much higher as many medical professionals do not know conscience protections exist, and pressure prevents others from coming forward.

In an online survey conducted on behalf of the CMA, 32 percent of faith-based health care professionals reported having "been pressured to refer a patient for a procedure to which [they] had moral, ethical or religious objections," and 20 percent of faith-based medical students polled said they are "not pursuing a career in obstetrics or gynecology because of perceived discrimination and coercion in that field."

Federal Conscience Protections

In response to mounting hostility to conscience rights, last December 19 [2008], President George W. Bush, through the Department of Health and Human Services (HHS), issued the Provider Conscience Regulation, which went into effect on January 20. It enforced existing federal conscience laws by requiring fund recipients to certify compliance and specifies a mechanism for investigating complaints.

The *New York Times* and other critics claimed the Bush provision constituted "sweeping new protections." But the regulation simply recited the underlying statutes verbatim and required fund recipients to promise to comply.

Less than two months later, President Obama, through HHS, released a directive to rescind the Bush rule, citing unsupported fears that it exceeded existing protection and could endanger access to care.

President Obama insists he is a "believer in conscience clauses." Speaking to Notre Dame graduates last May, he said, "Let's honor the conscience of those who disagree with abortion." But he qualified his statement, saying he wanted to "draft a sensible conscience clause, and make sure that all of our health care policies are grounded in clear ethics and sound science, as well as respect for the equality of women."

Citizens forced to pay into abortion-covering plans lose their conscience rights too.

What is Obama's definition of "sensible"? We asked Rep. Joe Pitts (R-PA) about what an Obama conscience clause would look like. Pitts, a leading pro-life critic of President Obama, said "anything that Obama produces is going to be suspect. He doesn't speak the whole truth. He's liable to come back with a clause full of loopholes."

Randy Pate, a political appointee at HHS who helped formulate the Bush conscience regulation, told us the Obama administration may have been surprised by the push-back against its efforts against conscience rights. (More than 340,000 people signed petitions in favor of the Bush regulations this March.) He thinks Obama "will wait until the broader health care reform debate dies down" before issuing his own conscience regulation.

The summer's health care reform debate thrust conscience rights into the foreground. In his speech to Congress on September 9, Obama said that "under our plan, no federal dollars will be used to fund abortions, and federal conscience protections will remain in place."

But even if Obama leaves federal conscience statutes "in place," those statutes may not apply to the vast new areas of regulation included in the bills. And to the extent that existing statutes do apply, Obama's rescission of the Bush regulation signals that his administration won't enforce them.

Government-Sanctioned Abortion

One of the biggest controversies in the health care debate concerned whether a government-run plan would cover abortion. Donna Harrison notes that to the extent that government expands or mandates abortion and other unethical practices, "there is more pressure to violate the Hippocratic Oath, and there will be more challenges on the basis of conscience."

Citizens forced to pay into abortion-covering plans lose their conscience rights too. Although the Hyde Amendment prevents many federal taxpayer dollars from funding abortions, it applies only to certain appropriations such as Medicare. In contrast, Obama has said that he considers "reproductive care," including abortion, to be "essential care" to be covered by his public insurance plan.

Under HR 3200, the House bill passed in the House Energy and Commerce committee in August, the public insurance plan would have covered abortion at taxpayers' expense. Likewise, the Senate bill offered by Sen. Max Baucus in September would have funded abortions through health care cooperatives.

Pro-life members of Congress from both parties saw the need to explicitly exclude abortion in the language of any reform bill. And no fewer than seven amendments (including four by Reps. Pitts and Bart Stupak [D-MI]) to ban government funding of abortion were proposed before the August recess. All were voted down.

Instead, Democrats offered a number of abortion funding "compromises." Congresswoman Lois Capps (D-CA) introduced an amendment that paid for abortion but claimed the payment came out of private premiums. But the National Right to Life and the U.S. [Conference of] Catholic Bishops opposed the arrangement as an accounting sleight of hand. Rep. Stupak called the proposal "a hidden abortion mandate."

To pro-life advocates, forcing participation in the moral evil of abortion violates doctors' duty to protect human life.

Government-sanctioned abortion coverage is unpopular. According to a 2008 Zogby poll, 71 percent of Americans do not want to pay for abortion nor have their employers provide health care that pays for abortion.

Public Opinion on Conscience Protections

Despite the long history and public opinion in favor of conscience protection, it is difficult to see how the debate will be resolved. Both sides have entrenched positions. From the perspective of abortion rights advocates, conscience rights erode a settled constitutional right that trumps all other interests. As Obama has said, "reproductive justice" is "one of the most fundamental rights we possess."

The Planned Parenthood Web site states that "it is unethical for health care providers to stand in the way of a woman's access to safe, legal and professional health care."

Abortion rights advocates are particularly concerned because groups like ACOG have warned that "the availability of abortion services is in jeopardy." According to the Guttmacher Institute, the number of abortion providers dropped from 2,908 in 1982 to 1,787 in 2005. And 87 percent of U.S. counties, including 31 percent of its metropolitan areas, have no abortion availability.

To pro-life advocates, forcing participation in the moral evil of abortion violates doctors' duty to protect human life. They argue that the real access issue involves the likely decrease in overall medical services as thousands of pro-life medical professionals are forced out of the profession. As Christian Medical Association CEO David Stevens, MD, stated about the Bush rule rescission, "Ultimately, it's just driving doctors with conscience issues out of practice."

In an April 2009 survey by the Polling Company/ WomanTrend, 87 percent of adults felt "it is important to make sure that health care professionals in America are not forced to participate in procedures and practices to which they have moral objections." Further, 95 percent of 2,865 faith-based health care professionals said, "I would rather stop practicing medicine altogether than be forced to violate my conscience."

Conscience Protections for Pharmacists

The anti-conscience movement has increasingly targeted pharmacists. According to Denise Burke of Americans United for Life, "The abortion lobby . . . recognize[s] that if [it] can establish legal precedent to coerce someone to violate their conscience regarding contraceptives, [it] can then easily extend that legal precedent to [RU-486], to coerce medical students to participate in abortion training, and to coerce doctors to participate in surgical abortion."

After abortion advocates convinced the Supreme Court to declare a fundamental right to contraception in 1965, *Roe v. Wade* followed relatively quickly in 1973.

In the 12 years since the Food and Drug Administration approved emergency contraception (EC) regimens, Planned Parenthood and the National Abortion Rights Action League (NARAL Pro-Choice America) have organized state campaigns to mandate EC dispensation. According to NARAL, "21 states have 32 laws and/or policies that improve women's access to EC."

A few states have enacted conscience clauses that protect pharmacists who choose not to dispense it. And some, paradoxically, have passed both.

But New Jersey exemplifies the trend with its 2006 law compelling dispensation not just of EC, but of all "legal" prescriptions. Because first- and even second-trimester abortions are increasingly performed by drugs like RU-486 and Cytotec, the New Jersey law is already an abortion mandate.

A Worsening Situation

The situation was not always this bad. Former HHS appointee Pate said, "For years after *Roe*, there was a general consensus that there is a right to abortion but no duty to be involved. That's why there was bipartisan support of conscience rights." The Church Amendment passed the Senate 92 to 1. Even the late Supreme Court Justice Harry Blackmun, author of *Roe v. Wade*, endorsed conscience clauses as "appropriate protection" for physicians and hospitals.

The American Medical Association's September journal for medical students states that "conscientious objection should be made when he or she chooses a specialty—not when he or she faces a patient." The article states that physicians must "concede moral authority [for conscience] to the legal system, a professional organization, or the informal consensus of one's peers."

Dr. Gene Rudd, senior vice president of the Christian Medical & Dental Associations, responded in an interview that "the primacy of patient care has always been the fundamental tenet of medical ethics."

Mary Jean Schumann, the American Nurses Association's [ANA's] chief programs officer, disagrees. "Nurses are there for the patient," she said in an e-mail response to our question about the ANA's position on conscience rights. "It's the patient's right to make decisions on care based on their beliefs, not the health care providers' beliefs."

When the Supreme Court made murder legal, it imposed an unprecedented conscience threat on the medical community.

Planned Parenthood lawyer Julie Cantor, MD, wrote in the *New England Journal of Medicine* in April that, "As the gatekeepers to medicine, physicians and other health care providers have an obligation to choose specialties that are not moral minefields for them. Qualms about abortion, sterilization and birth control? Do not practice women's health. . . . Conscience is a burden that belongs to the individual professional; patients should not have to shoulder it."

The Autonomy Rights of Patients

Opponents of conscience protection rally around the ideal of patient autonomy. Yet they ignore the autonomy rights of patients who want to visit pro-life doctors. In the [Polling Company/]WomanTrend poll, 88 percent of American adults surveyed said it is either very or somewhat important to them that they share a similar set of morals as their doctors, nurses, and other health care providers.

Future debates over conscience rights will be exacerbated by newly created technologies like cloning and embryonic stem cell research, as well as by the increase in surrogate motherhood and assisted suicide. The U.S. Conference of Catholic Bishops has stated, "As the range of medical technologies continues to expand, the number of medical services involving potentially serious conflicts of conscience is certain to increase."

The irony is that the government created the conscience crisis by abandoning its duty to protect human lives. When the Supreme Court made murder legal, it imposed an unprecedented conscience threat on the medical community.

The opposite right not to participate in abortion isn't just one competing interest among many. It is a plea from a uniquely important profession. If special interests are allowed to narrowly define "patient autonomy" and elevate it above the ideal of life preservation, then the medical profession can become one that mechanistically dispenses death.

Several times during this summer's health care fights, Barack Obama stated his desire that we "not get distracted by the abortion debate." But as their attacks on conscience rights intensify, Obama and his allies will ensure that abortion remains a distraction for the foreseeable future.

Organizations to Contact

The editors have compiled the following list of organizations concerned with the issues debated in this book. The descriptions are derived from materials provided by the organizations. All have publications or information available for interested readers. The list was compiled on the date of publication of the present volume; the information provided here may change. Be aware that many organizations take several weeks or longer to respond to inquiries, so allow as much time as possible.

Alliance to Defend Health Care
PO Box 301420, Boston, MA   02130
(617) 784-6367
e-mail: contact@defendhealth.org
Web site: www.massdefendhealthcare.org

The Alliance to Defend Health Care is a group of health care professionals and others who believe that health care is a fundamental human right and that the delivery of health care should be guided by science and compassion, not by corporate self-interest. The alliance collaborates with others to foster a broad public dialogue and health policy reforms to achieve universal access to high-quality, affordable health care for all. The Alliance to Defend Health Care has several resources available on its Web site, including "Principles of Health Care Delivery and Practice."

American Society of Law, Medicine & Ethics (ASLME)
765 Commonwealth Avenue, Suite 1634, Boston, MA   02215
(617) 262-4990 • fax: (617) 437-7596
e-mail: info@aslme.org
Web site: www.aslme.org

The American Society of Law, Medicine & Ethics (ASLME) is a nonprofit educational organization focused on the intersection of law, medicine, and ethics. ASLME aims to provide a forum to exchange ideas in order to protect public health, reduce health disparities, promote quality of care, and facilitate dialogue on emerging science. ASMLE publishes two journals: *Journal of Law, Medicine & Ethics* and *American Journal of Law & Medicine*.

Campaign for an American Solution

601 Pennsylvania Avenue NW, South Building, Suite 500
Washington, DC   20004
(202) 778-3200 • fax: (202) 331-7487
e-mail: info@americanhealthsolution.org
Web site: www.americanhealthsolution.org

Campaign for an American Solution is an initiative sponsored by America's Health Insurance Plans (AHIP), the national trade association for health insurance companies. The mission of the Campaign for an American Solution is to build support for workable health care reform based on core principles supported by the American people, and it works to facilitate a constructive conversation to that end. The campaign has press releases, letters to Congress, polling data, and other resources available on its Web site.

Center for Bioethics & Human Dignity (CBHD)

2065 Half Day Road, Deerfield, IL   60015
(847) 317-8180 • fax: (847) 317-8101
e-mail: info@cbhd.org
Web site: www.cbhd.org

The Center for Bioethics & Human Dignity (CBHD) works to bring explicit Christian engagement into the bioethics arena. CBHD works to equip thought leaders to champion the issues of bioethics using the tools of rigorous research, conceptual analysis, charitable critique, leading-edge publication, and effective teaching. Resources available at CBHD's Web site include reports and podcasts on topics such as bioethics, cloning, human enhancement, and stem cell research.

Center for Genetics and Society (CGS)

1936 University Avenue, Suite 350, Berkeley, CA   94704
(510) 625-0819 • fax: (510) 625-0874
e-mail: info@geneticsandsociety.org
Web site: www.geneticsandsociety.org

The Center for Genetics and Society (CGS) is a nonprofit information and public affairs organization working to encourage responsible uses and effective societal governance of the new human genetic and reproductive technologies. CGS works with scientists, health professionals, and civil society leaders to oppose applications of new human genetic and reproductive technologies that objectify and commodify human life and threaten to divide human society. CGS publishes articles, newsletters, and reports, including *Playing the Gene Card? A Report on Race and Human Biotechnology.*

Commonwealth Fund

1 East Seventy-fifth Street, New York, NY   10021
(212) 606-3800 • fax: (212) 606-3500
e-mail: info@cmwf.org
Web site: www.commonwealthfund.org

The Commonwealth Fund is a private foundation that aims to promote a high-performing health care system that achieves better access, improved quality, and greater efficiency, particularly for society's most vulnerable, including low-income individuals, the uninsured, minority Americans, young children, and elderly adults. The Commonwealth Fund carries out this mandate by supporting independent research on health care issues and initiating grants to improve health care practice and policy. The foundation publishes an annual report and the newsletter *The Commonwealth Fund Connection*, both of which are available on its Web site.

Council for Responsible Genetics (CRG)

5 Upland Road, Suite 3, Cambridge, MA   02140
(617) 868-0870 • fax: (617) 491-5344

e-mail: crg@gene-watch.org
Web site: www.councilforresponsiblegenetics.org

The Council for Responsible Genetics (CRG) is a nonprofit organization dedicated to fostering public debate about the social, ethical, and environmental implications of genetic technologies. CRG works through the media and concerned citizens to distribute accurate information and represent the public interest on emerging issues in biotechnology. CRG publishes *GeneWatch*, a magazine dedicated to monitoring biotechnology's social, ethical, and environmental consequences.

Ethics and Public Policy Center (EPPC)
1730 M Street NW, Suite 910, Washington, DC 20036
(202) 682-1200 • fax: (202) 408-0632
e-mail: ethics@eppc.org
Web site: www.eppc.org

The Ethics and Public Policy Center (EPPC) is dedicated to applying Judeo-Christian moral tradition to critical issues of public policy. Through its core programs, EPPC and its scholars work to influence policy makers and to transform the culture through the world of ideas. EPPC publishes the *New Atlantis*, a quarterly journal about technology with an emphasis on bioethics.

Euthanasia Research & Guidance Organization (ERGO)
24829 Norris Lane, Junction City, OR 97448-9559
(541) 998-1873
e-mail: ergo@efn.org
Web site: www.finalexit.org

The Euthanasia Research & Guidance Organization (ERGO) is a nonprofit organization that believes voluntary euthanasia, physician-assisted suicide, and self-deliverance are all appropriate life endings, depending on the individual medical and ethical circumstances. ERGO develops and publishes guidelines—ethical, psychological and legal—for patients and physicians to better prepare them to make life-ending decisions. Available at the ERGO Web site are videos, books, and essays, including the essay, "The Case for Physician-Assisted Suicide and Voluntary Euthanasia."

Genetics and Public Policy Center

Johns Hopkins University, Berman Institute of Bioethics
1717 Massachusetts Avenue NW, Suite 530
Washington, DC   20036
(202) 663-5971 • fax: (202) 663-5992
e-mail: gppcnews@jhu.edu
Web site: www.dnapolicy.org

The Genetics and Public Policy Center works to help policy makers, the press, and the public understand the challenges and opportunities of genetic medicine. The center conducts legal research and policy analysis, performs policy-relevant social science research, crafts policy recommendations, and influences national genetics policy. Available at the center's Web site are numerous testimony transcripts and reports, including "The Genetic Town Hall: Public Opinion About Research on Genes, Environment, and Health."

Georgetown Health Policy Institute

Georgetown University, 3300 Whitehaven Street NW
Suite 5000, Box 571444, Washington, DC   20057
(202) 687-0880 • fax: (202) 687-3110
Web site: ihcrp.georgetown.edu

The Georgetown Health Policy Institute is a multidisciplinary group of faculty and staff dedicated to conducting research on key issues in health policy and health services research. Institute members are engaged in a wide diversity of projects focusing on issues relating to health care financing, the uninsured, federal health insurance reforms, quality of care and outcomes research, mental health services research, and the impact of changes in the health care market on providers and patients. Publications sponsored by the institute include *Medicaid and State Budgets: Looking at the Facts.*

Hastings Center
21 Malcolm Gordon Road, Garrison, NY   10524-4125
(845) 424-4040 • fax: (845) 424-4545
e-mail: mail@thehastingscenter.org
Web site: www.thehastingscenter.org

The Hastings Center is a nonprofit bioethics research institute that works to address fundamental ethical issues in the areas of health, medicine, and the environment as they affect individuals, communities, and societies. The Hastings Center conducts research and education, and collaborates with policy makers to identify and analyze the ethical dimensions of their work. The Hastings Center publishes two periodicals: the *Hastings Center Report* and *IRB: Ethics & Human Research.*

Kennedy Institute of Ethics
Joseph and Rose Kennedy Institute of Ethics, Healy, 4th Floor
Georgetown University, Washington, DC   20057
(202) 687-8099 • fax: (202) 687-8089
Web site: kennedyinstitute.georgetown.edu

The Kennedy Institute of Ethics at Georgetown University is the world's oldest academic bioethics center. The Kennedy Institute is home to a group of scholars who engage in research, teaching, and public service on issues that include protection of research subjects, reproductive and feminist bioethics, end-of-life care, health care justice, intellectual disability, cloning, gene therapy, eugenics, and other major issues in bioethics. It publishes the *Kennedy Institute of Ethics Journal,* which offers a scholarly forum for diverse views on major issues in bioethics.

Physicians for a National Health Program (PNHP)
29 E. Madison, Suite 602, Chicago, IL   60602
(312) 782-6006 • fax: (312) 782-6007
e-mail: info@pnhp.org
Web site: www.pnhp.org

Physicians for a National Health Program (PNHP) is a nonprofit research and education organization of sixteen thousand physicians, medical students, and health professionals who support single-payer national health insurance. PNHP performs research on the need for fundamental health care system reform, coordinates speakers and forums, participates in town hall meetings and debates, contributes scholarly articles to peer-reviewed medical journals, and appears regularly on national television and news programs advocating for a single-payer system. Among the research papers sponsored by PNHP is *Illness and Injury as Contributors to Bankruptcy*.

United Network for Organ Sharing (UNOS)
700 North Fourth Street, Richmond, VA   23219
(804) 782-4800 • fax: (804) 782-4817
Web site: www.unos.org

United Network for Organ Sharing (UNOS) is a nonprofit, scientific and educational organization that administers the nation's only Organ Procurement and Transplantation Network (OPTN), established by the U.S. Congress in 1984. Through the OPTN, UNOS collects and manages data about every transplant event occurring in the United States; facilitates the organ matching and placement process; and brings together medical professionals, transplant recipients, and donor families to develop organ transplantation policy. UNOS publishes fact sheets, policy brochures, white papers, and the bimonthly magazine *Update*, all of which are available on its Web site.

Bibliography

Books

Carol Isaacson Barash	*Just Genes: The Ethics of Genetic Technologies.* Westport, CT: Praeger, 2008.
Tom L. Beauchamp and James F. Childress	*Principles of Biomedical Ethics*, 6th ed. New York: Oxford University Press, 2009.
Roberta M. Berry	*The Ethics of Genetic Engineering.* New York: Routledge, 2007.
Celia Deane-Drummond	*Genetics and Christian Ethics.* New York: Cambridge University Press, 2006.
Lisa A. Eckenwiler and Felicia G. Cohn, eds.	*The Ethics of Bioethics: Mapping the Moral Landscape.* Baltimore, MD: Johns Hopkins University Press, 2007.
Nancy Ehrenreich	*The Reproductive Rights Reader.* New York: New York University Press, 2008.
Sarah Franklin	*Dolly Mixtures: The Remaking of Genealogy.* Durham, NC: Duke University Press, 2007.
Karey Harwood	*The Infertility Treadmill: Feminist Ethics, Personal Choice, and the Use of Reproductive Technologies.* Chapel Hill, NC: University of North Carolina Press, 2007.

Hastings Center   *From Birth to Death and Bench to Clinic: The Hastings Center Bioethics Briefing Book for Journalists, Policymakers, and Campaigns.* Garrison, NY: Hastings Center, 2008.

Bruce R. Korf   *Human Genetics and Genomics.* Malden, MA: Blackwell, 2006.

H. Daniel Monsour, ed.   *Ethics and the New Genetics: An Integrated Approach.* Toronto, Ontario: University of Toronto Press, 2007.

Liza Mundy   *Everything Conceivable: How Assisted Reproduction Is Changing Our World.* New York: Anchor Books, 2008.

Ronald Munson, ed.   *Intervention and Reflection: Basic Issues in Medical Ethics,* 8th ed. Belmont, CA: Thomson Wadsworth, 2008.

Erik Parens, Audrey R. Chapman, and Nancy Press, eds.   *Wrestling with Behavioral Genetics: Science, Ethics, and Public Conversation.* Baltimore, MD: Johns Hopkins University Press, 2006.

Gregory E. Pence   *Classic Cases in Medical Ethics: Accounts of the Cases That Shaped and Define Medical Ethics,* 5th ed. New York: McGraw-Hill Higher Education, 2008.

Michael J. Sandel   *The Case Against Perfection: Ethics in the Age of Genetic Engineering.* Cambridge, MA: Belknap Press, 2007.

Periodicals

Rebecca Atkinson "I Wouldn't Have Minded if My Baby Had Been Born Deaf, but the Embryology Bill Insists I Should," *Guardian* (UK), October 10, 2008.

Scott W. Atlas "Rationing Health Care," *Forbes*, July 21, 2009.

Sharon Begley "Health-Care Rationing: Bring It On," *Newsweek*, September 2, 2009.

Lee Black and Robert M. Sade "Lethal Injection and Physicians: State Law vs. Medical Ethics," *Journal of the American Medical Association*, December 19, 2007.

Dan Brock "Rationing: Why It Is Ethical," *Health Care Cost Monitor*, July 16, 2009.

Nigel M. de S. Cameron "Outsourcing Birth: Let an Indian Woman Have Your Baby," *Christianity Today*, April 5, 2006.

Henry Chu "Wombs for Rent, Cheap," *Los Angeles Times*, April 19, 2006.

Gabriel M. Danovitch and Alan B. Leichtman "Kidney Vending: The 'Trojan Horse' of Organ Transplantation," *Clinical Journal of the American Society of Nephrology*, November 2006.

Veronica English "Is Presumed Consent the Answer to Organ Shortages? Yes," *British Medical Journal*, May 26, 2007.

Ellen Goodman   "The Ethical Failures of Fertility Treatment," *Boston Globe*, February 6, 2009. www.boston.com.

Viv Groskop   "The Real Causes of Infertility," *New Statesman*, July 5, 2007.

Amy Harmon   "Prenatal Test Puts Down Syndrome in Hard Focus," *New York Times*, May 9, 2007.

Laura Hershey   "Handicap Is Not a Death Sentence and Should Not Be Treated as One," *U.S. News & World Report*, August 10, 2009. www.usnews.com.

Benjamin Hippen   "The Case for Kidney Markets," *New Atlantis*, Fall 2006.

Arlie Hochschild   "Childbirth at the Global Crossroads," *American Prospect*, October 5, 2009.

Paul Hsieh   "The Free Market Is Not Another Form of Rationing," Pajamas Media, September 3, 2009.

Jeff Jacoby   "A Deadly Organ Donor System," *Boston Globe*, July 5, 2009.

Dick Lamm   "Better Health Care Through Rationing," *Huffington Post*, September 24, 2009. www.huffingtonpost.com.

Rory Leishman   "Physicians: Act on Your Convictions," *Catholic Insight*, November 2008.

David Leonhardt "Health Care Rationing Rhetoric Overlooks Reality," *New York Times*, June 17, 2009.

Larissa MacFarquhar "The Kindest Cut," *New Yorker*, July 27, 2009.

Betsy McCaughey "The Attack on Doctors' Hippocratic Oath," *Investor's Business Daily*, April 29, 2009. www.investors.com.

Gilbert Meilaender "Gifts of the Body," *New Atlantis*, Summer 2006.

Kevin B. O'Reilly "Other Nations, Other Answers: In Search of a Solution to the Organ Shortage," *American Medical News*, October 13, 2008. www.amednews.com.

Peggy Orenstein "Your Gamete, Myself," *New York Times Magazine*, July 15, 2007.

Clarence Page "Rationing Health Care," *Chicago Tribune*, August 9, 2009.

Virginia Postrel "...With Functioning Kidneys for All," *Atlantic*, July 9, 2009.

Sheldon Richman "The Market Doesn't Ration Health Care," Foundation for Economic Education, August 7, 2009.

Bonnie Rochman "The Ethics of Octuplets," *Time*, February 5, 2009.

Stephanie Saul "Birth of Octuplets Puts Focus on Fertility Clinics," *New York Times*, February 11, 2009.

John B. Shea   "Cardiac Arrest, Brain Death, and Organ Donation: The Inconvenient Truth," *Catholic Insight*, September 2007.

Rob Stein   "New Safety, New Concerns in Tests for Down Syndrome," *Washington Post*, February 24, 2009.

Michael D. Tanner   "Healthcare Is a Precious Commodity That Must Be Used Wisely," *U.S. News & World Report*, August 10, 2009.

Richard H. Thaler   "Opting In vs. Opting Out," *New York Times*, September 26, 2009.

Judith Warner   "Outsourced Wombs," *New York Times*, January 3, 2008.

Index